THE WOMEN *of* THE PASSION

KATHLEEN M. MURPHY

Liguori

LIGUORI, MISSOURI

Imprimi Potest: Thomas D. Picton, C.Ss.R.
Provincial, Denver Province • The Redemptorists

Nihil Obstat   *Imprimatur*
Philip J Kerr, S.T.L., V.G.   Keith Patrick Cardinal O'Brien
Censor Deputatus   Archbishop of Saint Andrews and Edinburgh
            4 January 2005

Previously published with the same title by St. Pauls Publishing, London, 2005.

ISBN 978-0-7648-1647-5

All biblical quotations taken from the *Revised Standard Version* (Catholic edition), Version 5, 1996 Christian Technologies, PO Box 2201, Independence, MO 64055. Available on CD by the Division of Christian Education, National Council for Churches in Christ, USA.

Excerpts from Pope John Paul II: "At the Beginning of the New Millennium *(Novo Millennio Ineunte)*" © 2001, and "Letter to Women" © 1995, reprinted with permission from Vatican Press, Libreria Editrica Vaticana. All rights reserved. Used with permission.

Excerpts from John Cardinal Ratzinger: "Letter to the Bishops of the Catholic Church on the Collaboration of Men and Women in the Church and in the World," reprinted with permission from Vatican Information Service, Libreria Editrice Vaticana. © 2004. All rights reserved. Used with permission.

Liguori Publications, a nonprofit organization, is an apostolate of the Redemptorists. To learn more about the Redemptorisits, visit Redemptorists.com.

Printed in the United States of America
11 10 09 08 07 5 4 3 2 1
First U.S. edition

Acknowledgments

This work would never have reached the publisher's desk if it had not been for the enthusiasm and genuine encouragement of the women and men who attended a series of lectures on "Women in Scripture" here at Saint Catharine's. I offer them my heartfelt thanks, and I hope that they will enjoy reading and discussing the additional material.

I am deeply indebted and immensely grateful to His Eminence Keith Patrick Cardinal O'Brien, Archbishop of Saint Andrews and Edinburgh, for his wonderful generosity and kindness in making time to write the Foreword to this little book, which aims to encourage an interest in Scripture, bring women and men to prayer, and support them in renewing their spirituality.

It gives me pleasure to offer my sincere thanks to my delightful niece, Irene Neville, who proofread my draft text and was always supportive and encouraging, and to Monsignor Philip Kerr, who kindly read the text.

I offer a very special word of thanks to my community and to the members of our Leadership Team for their consistent interest and partnership. Finally, I want to record my warmest thanks to Ms. Annabel Robson, the Commissioning Editor at St. Pauls who did so much to support me during the last weeks as we prepared to go to print; and to Sister Marie Henderson, R.S.M., of the Detroit Sisters of Mercy, for the beautiful cover image.

Contents

Foreword

I wish to warmly commend Sister Kathleen Murphy's book, *The Women of the Passion*. In his Apostolic Letter, At the Beginning of the New Millennium (*Novo Millennio Ineunte,* January 6, 2001), Pope John Paul II asked us all to contemplate the face of Christ through pondering the witness of sacred Scripture. One admirable way to do this is to reflect and in some way identify with the characters described as meeting the Lord in the course of his public ministry.

In telling the stories of the women whom we meet in the passion narrative, Sister Kathleen raises many questions on which we might reflect, questions that challenge us on how we today can bear witness to Christ. While this book might immediately appeal to women, it also has much to offer men. May the ideas contained herein help many to grow in union with Christ.

+ Keith Patrick Cardinal O'Brien

Cardinal Keith Patrick O'Brien
Archbishop of Saint Andrews and Edinburgh

Introduction

Lent is the special time of the year when we reflect on the passion of Jesus. During this season of grace, this year perhaps we could enrich ourselves and our spirituality by focusing on the passion through the stories of the women who either watched events from afar or who stood in a supporting role close to Jesus during his devastating ordeal. They fit into three categories: those women who were healed by Jesus physically and spiritually, those ordinary women who followed him because he gave them new vision and new hope, and his mother Mary. Each one had her own story and came to faith in Jesus because of her experience of him. Despite the opposition of the religious leaders of his day and the dictates of the Law, he ministered to each woman personally and as an individual. In gratitude for this, the women followed in empathy and partnership during his last horrific week. When we think of his passion and the women who were actively involved, we tend to think in terms of the immediate few days before his death on Good Friday. They were treacherous, tragic, and immensely painful days in which he experienced tremendous aloneness in terms of lack of intimate human friendship and empathy. They culminated in his death.

It is very important that we remember that Jesus' agony and passion did not just begin on Holy Thursday and conclude as a neatly wrapped package on Good Friday. From the moment he began his public ministry, his life was always under threat from the Pharisees, Sadducees, scribes, and Jewish leaders. Central to the reasoning behind the betrayal and death of Jesus was his ministry and his teaching through the beatitudes (Mt 5:3–12; Lk 6:20–25) and the corporal works of mercy (Mt 25:31–46). His authority for both was suspected and questioned. We read in Matthew and in Mark:

> *And when he entered the temple, the chief priests and the elders of the people came up to him as he was teaching, and said, "By what authority are you doing these things, and who gave you this authority?" Jesus answered them, "I also will ask you a question; and if you tell me the answer, then I also will tell you by what authority I do these things"* (Mt 21:23–24; Mk 11:28–29).

Simply stated, he was put to death because of his commitment to God's ministry of healing, caring for, and feeding the bodies, souls, and minds of God's people.

Unlike the women to whom he ministered, and from whom he received affirmation and support, and his chosen disciples, these men misunderstood his mission, misrepresented his teachings, and misappropriated the source of his miraculous powers. They misread his behavior and misinterpreted his words simply because they felt threatened in the social and religious position that they held within the community (Mt 23:1–12; Jn 7:7–13). They were dealing with a man who did not fit the mold into which they tried to imprison him. All of this was a tremendous source of physical strain and of emotional pain to him as he strove to be compassionate to all those in need, to teach those willing to listen, to care for the sick, and to share hospitality with the marginalized and with God's poor.

The fact that all three evangelists record that his mother, relatives, and friends were concerned for him demonstrates clearly the level of stress under which Jesus was working (Mt 12:46; Mk 3:31; Lk 8:20). His safety and good health were his mother's priority, as they would be the priority of any mother whose son was either overworking or in danger from an outside force or enemy. Despite the levels of fear created and instilled by the scribes, Pharisees, and Sadducees, and the threats that constantly faced him, women were among his most faithful disciples, supporters, and caregivers (Mt 27:55–56; Mk 15:40–42; Lk 23:28). However close his mother and all the women who had traveled with him during his ministry tried to be, there was no way that they could understand fully his inner struggles. The internal agony and grief that he experienced and carried in his mind and body on a daily basis were held privately and reverently at the core of his being. Despite this, he never let it interfere with his ministry to the most vulnerable in the society of his day.

It is not surprising that women were devoted to him because during his years of ministry he showed himself to be in solidarity with them. He readily ministered to them regardless of their faith persuasion, current spiritual and moral state, race, creed, culture, or social class (Jn 4:7–39). He cared for them in their sorrows (Lk 7:12–15), healed them in their sickness (Mt 9:20–22; Mk 7:22–29), forgave them in their sinfulness (Lk 7:37–50; 13:11–16), fed them when they were hungry (Mt 14:15–21), and shared meals with them in their homes (Lk 10:30–42).

Transcending the established norms of his own culture, Jesus treated women with openness, respect, acceptance and tenderness. In this way he honored the dignity which women have always possessed according to God's plan and in his love.[1]

He was there for them in their suffering, and he voluntarily suffered and accepted the unjust emotional and mental pain inflicted on him by the various religious groups in order to alleviate that of the women who needed to be unburdened physically and spiritually (Lk 13:11–17).

Because of this, his passion was an ongoing and an accelerating process throughout his public life until it climaxed on the Thursday of his final week and terminated in crucifixion the following day, the Friday that we call "Good." It would be a disservice to Jesus, to the individual women who are accounted for in the gospels, and to his mother if we did not make some effort to identify at least some of *"the women who had followed him from Galilee, stood at a distance, and saw these things"* (Lk 23:49), and the *"women who bewailed and lamented him,"* and to whom he said, *"Daughters of Jerusalem, do not weep for me, but weep for yourselves and for your children"* (Lk 23:27–28). As a body, all these women form the group to whom we give the title "The Women of the Passion." It was, in no small way, his ministry to these women that contributed so much to the register of unjust and conflicting evidence that his enemies gathered. This had been collected over a period of three years and was proudly presented to the Sanhedrin (Mk 14:53–64) and to the court of Pilate in the early hours of Friday morning following the Passover (Mk 15:1–5).

The women were there for him because he had been there for them. His ministry to them and to all those in need was unique. In light of this, it is right that we allow them to speak of him to us and to enlighten us as to why his service to them brought so much pain upon him, and why so many of them formed guards of honor, as it were, as he made his final journey to his death. Their stories will, hopefully, speak to us in our prayer, challenge us in our asceticism, arouse in us an attitude of gratitude, and bring peace to our souls. In addition, they will heighten our mission awareness and motivate us to good works in every area of our social relations and spirituality.

It is because of Jesus' transformation of them that these women have made their way into the gospels and the history of Christianity. As we, the women and men of this third millennium, struggle to live the gospel anew, let us permit them to support and to energize us this Lent, both as compassionate individuals, and as a community of faith, hope, and love. Their stories and their sufferings will teach us much about ourselves, our crosses, our social and emotional relationships, and our need for our God. Jesus changed their lives and made them whole. He will do the same for us if, like those named individuals who were there daily for him together with the anonymous groups of women from Galilee and Jerusalem, we open ourselves in faith to experience his healing, mercy, and compassion.

Kathleen M. Murphy

The Unnamed Woman Who Anointed Jesus at Bethany

MATTHEW 26:10–11

But Jesus, aware of this, said to them, "Why do you trouble the woman? For she has done a beautiful thing to me. For you always have the poor with you, but you will not always have me" (Mt 26:10–11).

THIS WOMAN FROM BETHANY had left the shadow of sin behind her and moved into the light because of her experience of Jesus. So strong had she become in her faith that she dared to gatecrash a party being given for Jesus in the house of Simon the leper. Her motive was not to be entertained but to render service. She was determined to honor Jesus in public. She appeared out of the shadow of the evening and entered a house that had an ambience of light and celebration. Her presence astonished all those present. Her story is told as part of the passion narrative in Matthew 26:6–13 and Mark 14:3–9. It is also recorded in Luke 7:36–50, but he uses the story to give a different teaching. John records the story too, and places it within six days of the passion. He modifies Matthew's and Mark's versions and names the woman as Mary (Jn 12:1–8). As a result, she is often thought of as Mary of Bethany, not to be confused with Mary Magdalene.

Here we will concentrate on the accounts given by Matthew and Mark. They tell us that Jesus was having a meal in the house of Simon the leper when a woman entered and poured an alabaster jar of expensive ointment over Jesus' head. Jesus was on a mission and so associating with sinners and outcasts. He was there not for his own pleasure but as a service to those who needed God's love and mercy. Scholars believe that the act of the woman was prophetic.[2] She was probably one of those who had heard Jesus tell the disciples, a few days earlier, that during their celebrations of the Passover the Son of Man would be crucified. Her action demonstrated that she recognized Jesus as the Son of Man—the Messiah—and that she was anticipating his predicted death. Mark writes,

It was now two days before the Passover and the feast of Unleavened Bread. And the chief priests and the scribes were seeking how to arrest him by stealth, and kill him; for they said, "Not during the feast, lest there be a tumult of the people" (Mk 14:1–2).

It is at that point that he inserts the story of this generous prophetess. He has set the scene and he has a unique story to tell. Both he and Matthew tell us that the woman anointed the head of Jesus. Anointing of the head would have been a well-known ritual to all Jews who were familiar with the Old Testament. It was seen as a symbol of leadership. Kings, priests, and prophets were anointed. The reason for anointing was to make people and things sacred. McKenzie tells us that it was done to priests, tents of meeting, the Ark, and the furniture of the tent.[3] The woman was possibly making the point to all present that she recognized Jesus as the Messiah and was inviting them to do likewise. Oil was used in anointing ceremonies and it ritualized the community's willingness to follow the guidance of a selected person as a leader. "…Anointing brings the spirit of Yahweh upon the person and impels him to some extraordinary deed: but even where it is not mentioned, anointing made the person a charismatic officer whose mission could be executed under the impulse of the spirit."[4] Saul was anointed by Samuel (1 Sam 10:1 ff) and David was anointed (1 Sam 16:13), to mention just two kings who were leaders of their people. It is not a ritual that was used widely in the New Testament. We read about it in James 5:14 in terms of healing and the forgiveness of sins. This is a ritual with which all Catholics are familiar in the sacrament of the sick.

We can be forgiven for wondering if the anointing by the woman further enraged the Jews who were present, as well as their leaders, and actually hastened the forthcoming death of Jesus. Her silence, behavior, and action certainly challenged everyone present in the house. Scripture goes on to tell us that even some of Jesus' own disciples questioned the use of the precious ointment—pure nard.

But there were some who said to themselves indignantly, "Why was the ointment thus wasted? For this ointment might have been sold for more than three hundred denarii, and given to the poor." And they reproached her (Mk 14:4–5).

Despite their closeness to Jesus and the fact that he had warned them of his forthcoming destruction, none of his male disciples appears to have anticipated what the woman's anointing might have signified, or indeed, the horrendous events of the next three days and the rush that would have to take place in order to bury his body before the onset of the Jewish Sabbath. Sue and Larry Richards, in commenting on her action state, "Since the women were among His disciples, it is possible that she knew exactly what she was doing."[5] Like many of us in ministry, they were so carried away with what they were currently involved in that they were out of touch with the surrounding reality. They only heard, from what Jesus said, what they were ready to entertain. Like so many of us too, they lived in the present and only understood in retrospect.

Matthew tells us that Judas responded to her action by going to the chief priests to hand Jesus over to them. He, unlike this nameless woman, had money in mind. He offered Jesus at a price. They paid him and he looked for a convenient moment to hand him over. Meanwhile, the woman responded to the mutterings and outright attack of the disciples and others with a dignified silence. Ever conscious of his duty to uphold social justice and to affirm virtue, Jesus, in recognition of her love, faith, and generosity, defended her.

> *Jesus said, "Let her alone; why do you trouble her? She has done a beautiful thing to me. For you always have the poor with you, and whenever you will, you can do good to them; but you will not always have me. She has done what she could; she has anointed my body beforehand for burying. And truly, I say to you, wherever the gospel is preached in the whole world, what she has done will be told in memory of her"* (Mk 14:6–9).

"Historically women's work has usually gone unnoticed and unrewarded. Jesus sets himself against the injustice."[6] Jesus advised them that the anointing was in anticipation of his burial, and some scholars see it as a type of *extreme unction.*[7] Many Catholics find great consolation in this thought, as they contemplate their own demise. For Jesus, this was to be the only anointing he would receive. It was performed

4

for him by a woman. She was the only one among the close followers who had the initiative, vision, and courage to take an appropriate, and an extravagant, action. By their very nature women are creative, generous, and perceptive. These are qualities that are essential to life-giving motherhood and community building. As one of our foremothers in faith, this nameless woman represented all women in mercy, love, and in faith.

Many people who receive the sacrament of the sick speak afterward of the peace and tranquillity that they experience as a result of the sacrament. This healing action of God in the soul probably had a similar uplifting effect on Jesus who certainly appreciated and affirmed it. It is interesting that the anointing was administered by a woman. We have to ask ourselves if it might be possible that there is a message here for the Church in this third millennium. "Jesus does not speak of any other disciple, not even Peter, or a James or a John, in the glowing terms he uses for this woman."[8] Her action was generosity at its best. It was an act of love and reverence of unique importance and significance. *And truly, I say to you, [said Jesus], wherever the gospel is preached in the whole world, what she has done will be told in memory of her*" (Mk 14:9).

The woman did not need to defend herself, or to use control, or power mechanisms to win herself a place in history. Her worth was noted by Jesus, and all those who followed her in Christianity would read her epitaph. It was written by Jesus, and it stands out in the pages of Scripture for our inspiration and edification. She gave all she had while her male observers, following the example of their predecessors who fifteen hundred years earlier had murmured against and attacked Moses in the desert, murmured and criticized Jesus now as he—the new Moses—was about to take the final step in leading them into—a "new land"—the New Covenant.

Reflection

The scene for this story was Bethany—the home of lepers, the ritually impure, and those shadowed by sin. The woman understood the area and its ethos. She had once been shadowed by sin herself, but now she walked and worked enlightened by divine grace. She was up-front. She was going to share the light with others and to challenge them to do likewise. In her silence she had a message for everyone present and for all succeeding generations. They might reject it. But she would not be frightened into holding it in private. Her extravagant action does not make economic sense. But the gospel is not about fiscal economics. It is about the economics of love and compassion.

Generally speaking, when the gospel is fully embraced it offers us more than enough asceticism during Lent and there is little, if any, need for us to take on additional sacrifices as our selected way of doing penance. Someone once said, very wisely, that our Creator is not so much interested in the mortifications we select for ourselves as in "observing" how we respond to those presented to us in our everyday life through our own misguided decision, the people with whom we live and work, the needs of our church, and through the situations in which we find ourselves but that are beyond our control. Frequently when we choose additional forms of mortification during Lent, it is our own egos we are boosting as opposed to living a life modeled on the economy of generosity displayed by the woman from Bethany, and in conformity to the beatitudes (Mt 5:3–12; Lk 6:20–25) and the corporal works of mercy (Mt 25:31–46).

As we proceed on our Lenten pilgrimage, are we conscious of the shadow side of our own lives? Do we realize that we are called on to reject it and with this woman to move into the light that is Jesus? Do we realize that the closer to that light we get, the more our shadowed past will shrink away and we will become new creations? Are we aware that our shadow is at its longest when we have faced our backs to Jesus?

- When it comes to considering our wealth and resources, which are we most surely motivated by: the storing up of money and the acquisition of property in order to be secure in a future over which we have no control and might never live to see, or by embracing those who appear to us to live in the shadows, and those who are either unknown to or unrecognized by our social services?

- Do we realize that many children and young people today are forced into the shadows because of the shadows in which their parents live and have brought them up?

The young learn how to live in the light in the home; there they learn the value of life and the gift of the sacraments. Parents who have received forgiveness are better able to extend it to their children and teach the value of reconciliation. Broken homes and homes with addicted parents frequently speak loudly of shadow or a lack of forgiveness. The young with little experience of reconciliation only know anger, resentment, and bitterness. They tend to live what they experience; with no positive experiences of forgiveness, they feel the only way forward is to embrace the shadow. This devours them. In this reflection, we focus our prayer on dysfunctional homes, fractured families, and on victims of Satanism and suicide.

- Are we aware that these are scourges in our current society? If so, how frequently do we submit them to Jesus in our prayer and plead with him to extend his anointing hands on them?

- Are we aware that when we live with guilt even if we have been forgiven, we are still in shadow? Do we realize that God does not look back at our mistakes and our sins? Are we aware that regardless of how sinful we have been we are made in the image of God, that we were enrolled as sons and daughters at baptism, and that God's invitation during this life is always into the sun, and in the life to come, to the paschal banquet to be anointed not by Mary of Bethany but by the Son himself?

Caiaphas' Maidservants Who Challenged Peter

MATTHEW 26:69
MARK 14:66–72
LUKE 22:56–62
JOHN 18:25–27

THE SECOND WOMAN (or pair of women) presented to us by the evangelists are featured in the courtyard of Caiaphas' house.

Now Peter was sitting outside in the courtyard. And a maid came up to him, and said, "You also were with Jesus the Galilean" (Mt 26:69).

For a second time in the passion narratives we are presented with a nameless woman, or in Matthew's case, nameless women. All four evangelists record this particular incident. It clearly made a huge impression on all the followers and on all those who preached the good news in the infant church. Peter is presented here as weak and cowardly, but thankfully, human. All those hearing the story of his three denials and knowing the relationship that existed between him and Jesus prior to this incident would, in their minds, immediately contrast the fidelity of Jesus to Peter with the infidelity of Peter to Jesus. All Matthew's Jewish listeners and readers would have understood the deep significance of the fact that the denial was threefold, that it became more adamant each time, and that the final witness to it was a man. Having been brought up in the Jewish culture, they would have known that the testimony of a woman would have been viewed as implausible. The word of a man posed no problems. One man's evidence was believed to be more trustworthy than that of a multitude of women.

In reflecting spiritually on this painful and traumatic episode, we see that initially a mere slip of a girl, a servant to the high priest, one without status of influence, who held one of the lowliest positions in the household—that of doorkeeper—was able to scare the man who saw himself as robust and fearless. This simple maid had been able to frighten Peter into denying the friend he had so recently vowed to defend, even if it meant having to die.[9] Now that he was at his most vulnerable and without the support of his peers, he lost courage. There was no one there who knew him. He could just be Peter, the fragile human being. There was no need to be the rock when neither Jesus nor his peers were there to witness that he, too, was a son of Eve.

Peter had been the one who had identified Jesus as the Son of God (Mt 16:15–16; Mk 8:29). He had been selected to be present at the transfiguration and had heard the voice from heaven claiming Jesus as the beloved Son who was commissioned as a teacher (Mt 17:1–8). He had been chosen by Jesus to be the rock on which the Church would be built (Mt 16:18). Just as his faithlessness is recorded by all four evangelists so, too, is the profession of faith in which he had sworn undying loyalty to Jesus only days previously (Mt 26:33; Mk 14:29; Lk 22:33; Jn 13:37). These professions of fidelity, by Peter, would have impressed those listening to the gospel message and given them courage in times of trial, hardship, and persecution, and they would have been experiencing plenty of that.

So what might have been their reaction when they heard the next installment of the story of the faith and fidelity of the man who had been chosen to lead the taking of the good news to the ends of the earth? The message being preached to them was one of mercy, compassion, and forgiveness. They would already have had a good grasp of these virtues and that would have stood them in good stead to face this trauma. But their evangelists would have had to go on; this was not the end of Peter's failing his master. The denial continued. Either that maidservant returned to challenge Peter again, or as Matthew records, a second woman came along who also worked for the high priest (Mt 26:7; Lk 22:58), who challenged Peter. In keeping with Jewish legislation regarding witnesses and the need for three, Matthew is probably correct in his recording of the incident. Again Peter denied any knowledge of Jesus. This latter woman would have had no higher status than the first. She was possibly the fire stoker. But she would have had a loyalty to her master, and she would be proud of the fact that she had any part in the household. Her priority would have been to glean information for her master, and her loyalty would have matched that professed by Peter to Jesus only days previously. Jesus was the master's enemy and in consequence hers too.[10]

Finally a male bystander challenged Peter. This time Peter's denial was made with force matching only his protestations of undying loyalty a few days before. However, the drama took on a totally new message and emotion for the listeners when their evangelists introduced the next character, action, and reaction in tragedy.

Three of the evangelists record simply that the cock crowed at the very moment of the third denial. On hearing it Peter remembered what Jesus had foretold and, in a state of pure devastation, he went out and wept bitterly in repentance. This was not the action of a man who had lost faith. It was the behavior of one who had experienced mercy and recognized that forgiveness was available to all those who acknowledged their need. Luke's account is more moving. He adds that Jesus turned and looked at Peter who, seeing his master's gaze, broke down. Listeners would have empathized with Peter and recognized their own human frailty and need for forgiveness. This story would probably have affirmed rather than weakened their faith. The image of repentance is powerful and it is greatly enriched by Luke's additional detail. Mercy looked into the face of one who cried out for mercy that equaled loving compassion.

The authors of *The New Jerome Biblical Commentary* point out that the threefold denial was not without purpose. "In Jewish moral theology of apostasy during persecution a private denial was less grave than a public one, and an evasive denial was less grave than an explicit one."[11] Mark's account of the denials is a gradual buildup to an explicit denial. This was a most serious sin. The important point is that Peter recognized his offense and the gravity of it and took appropriate action. The nameless woman/women here are very important. They are insignificant and fragile but they have power. That power was capable of bringing the man who appeared to be Jesus' most loyal and staunch follower to his knees. They caught a proud man off-guard. They exposed human frailty and they demonstrated to Peter himself, and to all succeeding generations, that perseverance in virtue is never to be taken for granted. It is a grace—one to be prayed for daily. They had established that women have power regardless of position. They had made it clear that the tongue is a dangerous weapon, and that there are grave risks involved in unreflective or idle communication. They had raised the red flag to all those tempted to be overly self-righteous and self-reliant. Furthermore, their power over Peter was to stand as a warning to all those in vowed commitments, and in situations of trust, that we are only earthen vessels and ultimately utterly dependent for perseverance on our God, who is mercy.

Reflection

Just as the maid(s) served Caiaphas, we, too, are in service. As Peter was a disciple of Jesus, we are disciples too. We can therefore put ourselves in both positions but we must first make one distinction. We did not apply for a job and we are not paid as was Caiaphas' staff. Having been anointed in baptism we, like Peter, have been chosen to walk in the footsteps of prophets, priests, and kings. We are commissioned members of God's household. We are called to represent and to present the good news of mercy and compassion by the way we live, act, and speak.

- ✺ Do we sit quietly in the Messiah's courtyard keeping ourselves comfortable while God's poor are suffering, while women and children are abused and marginalized?

- ✺ Are we genuinely committed to living the gospel consciously, not just during the few weeks of Lent but holistically and through the whole of life's journey?

- ✺ Do we swear to be agents of mercy and justice while watching local councils, governments, and world leaders engage in repressive or capitalist endeavors that increase the already unbearable burdens on those forced to become transit camp migrants, victims of racism, and hostages to drug addiction, prostitution, and pornography?

- ✺ When Jesus looks into our hearts and faces this Lent, does he see women and men who are genuine partners in mercy and willing to expose evil and promote mercy regardless of its social, emotional, or physical cost?

Pilate's Wife

MATTHEW 27:19

NOW WE TURN to the third nameless woman who is featured in Jesus' passion, the wife of Pilate and an outsider to Judaism like the Samaritan woman at the well (Jn 4:7–38; Mk 15:40).

While he was sitting on the judgment seat, his wife sent word to him, "Have nothing to do with that righteous man, for I have suffered much over him today in a dream" (Mt 27:18–19).

Unlike the "insignificant" woman or women who engaged and exposed Peter during Jesus' trial before Caiaphas, this woman had status and a certain degree of legitimate influence as the wife of the Roman governor. She was inspired to command her husband to act justly. "Have nothing to do with this just man" is much more than a request or a plea. Only Matthew mentions Pilate's wife, and he simply devotes one line to her involvement in the passion. Scholars believe that her dream represents "a redactional insertion." Dreams in Matthew represent divine guidance. Here the message that Jesus is "just" suggests that he should be released.[12] The one line allocated to Pilate's wife por-

14

trays her as a woman of determination, action, integrity, industry, and strength. Her intervention was to single her out among the women disciples of Jesus.

Like the nameless woman of Bethany, she was left with no need for admirers to erect a tombstone in her memory. By sending one simple message of warning to her husband, she went down in the pages of Scripture and in the history of Christendom for the edification of all generations. That one simple message would have challenged Pilate at the very root of his being. It is recorded in Scripture because of its importance. It challenged Pilate then, and it continues to speak to and to challenge all succeeding generations.

The country's most powerful man was sitting in judgment. Pilate was the only one who could pass a sentence on Jesus (Jn 18:31). Because of his position and the publicity that the ministry of Jesus had attracted, he would have known quite a lot about him. He and his wife would have heard the positive as well as the negative reports on Jesus. Together in the privacy of their home they would have discussed them over the years, and they would have had their own views on the caring teacher who was also a miracle worker. In light of this, Pilate had grave doubts about the guilt of the accused, because Matthew states, *"He knew it was out of envy that they had delivered him up"* (Mt 27:18). Luke tells us that he tried to avoid giving a judgment by sending Jesus to Herod, who had jurisdiction in Galilee where Jesus had begun his ministry. To his dismay and to that of his wife too, Herod returned Jesus to him for judgment and sentencing. It was possibly as she looked out from her window that Pilate's wife saw the rabble return and realized that Jesus was in grave danger. Her womanly instinct would have been to try to protect the innocent. She had to act in haste if she was to influence her husband, calm his concern, and affirm him in his conviction that Jesus was guiltless.

Her message only heightened his concern and increased his reservations about the guilt attributed to Jesus. *"Have nothing to do with that righteous man, for I have suffered much over him today in a dream"* (Mt 27:19). She had confirmed to Pilate that Jesus was innocent. The words "this righteous man" must have echoed in his ears as he made a last attempt to bargain with the Jews. Immersed in the Old Testament, Matthew would have understood the significance of dreams to his Jewish listeners. For Matthew and for his addressees, Pilate's wife would have been God's messenger. She said that she had suffered much on account of Jesus. Emotionally, she was drained. Intellectually, she was baffled, and spiritually, she was shattered. She knew an injustice was being done. She was not asking for mercy. There was no need for that. She was speaking about a man whom she and her husband had already agreed privately to be innocent. She was asking for the lesser virtue of justice.

According to Mary Anne Getty Sullivan, suffering much is a mark of discipleship in Mark's Gospel. "But this is not suffering for suffering's sake. Pilate's wife appears to want her suffering to be meaningful, to at least ensure that she and her husband do what they can to avoid complicity in the death of Jesus."[13] She tried to persuade Pilate at least to act justly regardless of the consequences. Fearing his wife's reaction if he failed to heed her command, he made a final effort to appease the Jews and to free himself of culpability. He offered them a deal that he hoped would at least spare him from having to sentence Jesus to death. He was unsuccessful. His wife's command had been in vain. She was Jesus' sole advocate. She had been inspired by God to command that innocence be respected, but the cries of the powerful triumphed over her. "…[H]er voice was not strong enough to overcome the forces of evil represented by the corrupt priests and elders, who had taken counsel against Jesus to put Him to death."[14]

"Have nothing to do with that righteous man," she had commanded. Pilate hesitated on receiving the message. He reflected hastily but de-

cided that if he was to continue in his position as governor, he had to do something, so he took some water and washed his hands, telling the Jews, *"I am innocent of this man's blood; see to it yourselves"* (Mt 27:24). Was this his way of attempting to obey his wife's command, or was it his way of trying to ease his own conscience? That his wife's message touched him deeply was clearly obvious in his speech and in his behavior. But other influences such as his need for power and position proved more powerful, and the innocent was led away to be crucified.

Tradition states that Pilate's wife became a follower of Jesus, but in secret, and that her name was Claudia. A follower here may, in the initial stages, simply mean an admirer. It is very possible that seeing the events that followed the crucifixion she came to faith. In the belief that she was gifted with faith, she is reverenced by the Greek Ortho-dox Church as a saint and her feast is celebrated on October 27. Many people believe that the trouble, of which Pilate's wife had spoken in her message to him, eventually fell on him. History records that his governorship terminated unexpectedly, he was exiled, and he com-mitted suicide. His wife's plea that he should have nothing to do with a *"just man"* must have haunted him. His own attempts to tell himself that he was free from guilt in the words *"I am innocent of this man's blood; see to it yourselves"* (Mt 27:24b) were his way of trying to con-vince himself that he was not guilty. Efforts to convince himself that he was innocent must have obsessed him for the rest of his life. He knew that he had ignored an enlightened plea and gone against his own conscience. He had let his political position and need for status interfere with his moral judgment, and it is reasonable to believe that he lived to regret it.

Reflection

Pilate's wife had a heart. During this Lent, that heart pleads to be allowed to touch the hearts of those who seek truth and justice, and members of Western governments and armed forces involved in wars in areas such as Palestine/Israel, Iraq, and Afghanistan. Her intervention on Jesus' behalf challenges us in terms of our reaction to injustices inflicted on those who cannot defend themselves.

- ❧ Are we "heart people" when faced with injustice in our homes, parishes, local areas, and in national and international politics? If we are, what action do we take in an effort to secure that justice which alone can bring peace?

- ❧ Do we register our objections to injustice by letter, phone, electronic mail, the press, or by participating in group representations organized by others?

- ❧ Are we advocates of justice to the point where it impinges on our own liberty, resources, and spirituality, or are we, like Pilate, people who look for an easy way out? If we don't find it do we, metaphorically speaking, wash our hands and tell ourselves that it is other people's business?

- ❧ Where are we when the needs for affordable housing, necessary child benefits, fair pensions, and reasonable levels of taxation are being discussed?

- ❧ Jesus was terrorized by his enemies, and Pilate's wife could see that. As we journey through Lent this year, do we recognize that war and poverty are the swamps in which terrorism breathes? If we do, what action are we taking to alert misguided capitalist governments to the injustices of their activities in third-world countries?

The Women of Jerusalem

IN CONSIDERING THIS GROUP of self-giving and faithful followers, it will enrich our Lenten prayer if we divide this group into two
units. We will consider first the general body and then focus on two
special women who had a particular reason to be part of the group and
whose stories speak of conversion and mission to us at a time in our
Christian community when we need to pray for a radically new vision
in these areas.

> *But Jesus turning to them said, "Daughters of Jerusalem, do not weep
> for me, but weep for yourselves and for your children"* (Lk 23:28).

The gospel accounts of the passion of Jesus make very clear that
the male disciples deserted him and fled in fear (Mk 14:50). Likewise,
they each document the presence and fidelity of women (Mt 27:55; Mk
15:40; Lk 23:49b).

While they are unanimous in confirming the fidelity and empathy
of women, they vary in their accounts of those who took an active role
in conveying their loyalty and distress, as well as in the positions they

took up, from the moment when he was presented to Caiaphas to the moment when Jesus died on the cross.

Some evangelists name certain women and overlook others. Scholars believe that this is because protocol only allowed for the naming of those who held leading positions in the community, or in this case, in the discipleship.[15] Many are not named. This may be accounted for by the fact that in the androcentric environment in which Jesus lived and operated women were generally recognized in terms of their husband, as in Pilate's wife (Mt 27:19); their father, as in Jarius' daughter (Lk 8:40–42); or some other male relative, as in the mother of the sons of Zebedee (Mt 20:20). It would appear from the gospels that there were only about nine women in leading positions in the discipleship. (Incidentally, the gospels name only twenty-four men.)

Luke introduces us to the first group of women who presented themselves to Jesus on his route to Calvary:

And there followed him a great multitude of the people, and of women who bewailed and lamented him. But Jesus turning to them said, "Daughters of Jerusalem, do not weep for me, but weep for yourselves and for your children. For behold, the days are coming when they will say, 'Blessed are the barren, and the wombs that never bore, and the breasts that never gave suck!' Then they will begin to say to the mountains, 'Fall on us'; and to the hills, 'over us.' For if they do this when the wood is green, what will happen when it is dry?" (Lk 23:27–31)

In this case, these daughters of Jerusalem represented professional mourners prescribed in Jewish custom to accompany the corpse to burial. They are not the women who had followed him from Galilee and were partners in ministry with him (Lk 23:27).[16] They were, rather, those who had been ministered to, or been friends of women and their families who had received mercy from Jesus. They were the grateful and the faithful of their day. Luke knew that suffering weakens faith, so here he is using Jesus' words to the women to encourage all those who suffer to live and pray in the presence of God who understands pain.

Traditionally in Scripture a woman was considered truly blessed when she gave birth. In Genesis 1:28, the instruction from the Creator is to be fruitful. Now these faithful and faith-filled women are hearing a different message. Those from the membership who lived long enough after Jesus to experience the reign of Titus in AD 70 "would remember his words about the barren being blessed when they saw babies delivered up to the knife."[17]

By recording Jesus' words to this group of women, Luke eternalized them just as Matthew had immortalized the woman from Bethany, Caiaphas' maidservants, and Pilate's wife. The portrait painted by Luke is poignant, and it touches the hearts of all who picture it in meditation. *"They bewailed and lamented him."* These women of Jerusalem, the holy city, genuinely grieved with the one who was holy. They recognized that a grave injustice had been inflicted on a *"just man"* (Mt 27:19). The Jews led Jesus straight from Pilate's court to Calvary. They were in a hurry because they had to have him buried before the onset of the Sabbath, which was fast approaching. There is a journey and an urgency involved here. Both are typical of Luke's writing.

After Jesus' conception Mary went in haste to a town in the hill country of Judea (Lk 1:39). On the way to Calvary, the soldiers seized a man to help Jesus. *Seized* is a hurried action that equates with grabbing quickly and indiscriminately. There is urgency here. The whole of the passion narrative is one of hasty action. There is neither thinking nor planning time. This applied to the women, too. They would have heard the news of Jesus' arrest from their menfolk and made snap decisions to be there for him. They were taking a risk, but they did not worry about the gamble. After all, he had always been there for them and it was because of his ministry to them and to others who needed mercy that he was now carrying the crossbar of the gibbet on which he would shortly die. Seeing him brutally violated was devastating for them. They knew that he was being crucified because of the evil in the hearts of the proud, the insecure, and the corrupt.

The Jews might have been in a hurry. However, Jesus was not. He had always paced himself and he was not going to change to make things easy for his persecutors. He was still in ministry and he would continue that service to the end. He noticed the grieving women, and he stopped. He spoke to them. The prophecy that had been made by Simeon in the Temple thirty-three years earlier was being fulfilled. He was destined to be a sign that would be rejected (Lk 2:34). The women were the witnesses to that rejection.

He addressed them as "Daughters of Jerusalem"—a form of address they would have recognized. It was frequently used in their Old Testament Scriptures in situations of both joy and grief. In this instance, it is certainly spoken in terms of sorrow. The sorrow is for the women of Jerusalem whose faith and faithfulness Jesus is affirming in speaking to them but for whose future he is laden with grief. He could see what lay ahead of them in the city that should have been a holy place but which, sadly, had a history of corruption and injustice. It was the place about which Jesus earlier had lamented when he said,

"O Jerusalem, Jerusalem, killing the prophets and stoning those who are sent to you! How often would I have gathered your children together as a hen gathers her brood under her wings, and you would not!" (Mt 23:37)

On his way to Calvary, he was possibly thinking again about all the grave injustices that had come from that city, and verbalizing, in shaded language, the destruction that he could foresee being visited upon it and its people because of their own sinfulness. We read in the prophecy of Jeremiah:

And the people to whom they prophesy shall be cast out in the streets of Jerusalem, victims of famine and sword, with none to bury them—them, their wives, their sons, and their daughters. For I will pour out their wickedness upon them (Jer 14:16).

Less than forty years after the crucifixion the Temple in Jerusalem was destroyed, and the city's people would never again be in a position to rebuild it.

Jesus concluded his address to the daughters of Jerusalem with an ancient proverb,

Then they will begin to say to the mountains, "Fall on us"; and to the hills, "Cover us." For if they do this when the wood is green, what will happen when it is dry? (Lk 23:30–31)

His precise meaning here is unclear. In light of what the Jews and the Romans have done to Jesus, some scholars attempt an explanation as follows: "For if they have done this to Jesus, one who is life-giving, what will happen to dead unrepentant Jerusalem?"[18]

Luke sent Jesus on a journey, from Pilate's court in Jerusalem, out of the city to the hill of Calvary. Jesus was liberated from Jerusalem by the time he met the women. He was free from the evil of power seekers. He was available to give new hope to those who were receptive. The women were there for him and ready to embrace his message. They were with him in his new vision. They would give birth to the next generation and ensure that God's people were not left behind. They would form the womb of a Judaism that would be life-giving because it was born in justice and mercy outside Jerusalem.

Reflection

In our day we form the womb for a renewed vision in a Western world where our faith is being marginalized and diluted. Through us it has the possibility of being reborn and taken out afresh beyond today's "Jerusalem" to a world starved of a faith-filled spirituality. We live in a world where our sisters and brothers—the *green* in terms of the young and the *dry* in terms of the old—are under threat. Many are abused by those who should be their caregivers. Many have their lives terminated before they can begin to survive independently. Many have their span of life planned out for them and in so-called mercy it is terminated when they cease to be useful or become a burden to those who once depended on them for sustenance and who should be their protectors.

- As we reflect on current-day issues during Lent, is Jesus speaking to us, and if he is, what is his message? As the womb of Christianity in the third millennium, is he inviting us to meet him outside Jerusalem in order to renew and rekindle his message of mercy?

- Where are we when the issues of euthanasia, abortion, famine and war relief, and third-world debt are being legislated on?

- Do we know what is going on in our cities today, not just in our heads, but in our hearts? Do we allow our heads and hearts to motivate us to action on behalf of the "Jesus" who is being crucified in our midst?

- Are we there for him who was and who is there for us? Does Jesus notice us as, liturgically, we prepare to remember and ritualize his passion?

The Woman Found Committing Adultery

JOHN 8:3–11

HERE WE MEET a woman who, on behalf of all those who received a second chance from Jesus, had reason to mourn his sufferings.

Jesus looked up and said to her, "Woman, where are they? Has no one condemned you?" She said, "No one, Lord." And Jesus said, "Neither do I condemn you; go, and do not sin again" (Jn 8:10–11).

This story, which is so Lukan in imagery and in terms of Jesus' compassionate, forgiving, and merciful relationships with women (Lk 7:37; 8:43; 10:38; 13:11–16), appears only in John, the gospel of life, light, and love. It is one of only two stories relating specifically to sinful women recorded in John's Gospel (Jn 4:5–30; 8:3–11). Both have a paschal dimension to them, and as samples of the *"many other things which Jesus did"* (Jn 21:25) and which he taught during his ministry, they support the holistic vision that John portrays of Jesus in his writings. Both stories demonstrate that Jesus worked with the marginalized. His was a model of ministry that percolated upward. Consequently, judgments were always made on him that would surface again during his passion. The charge against this woman is a reminder that he was always on trial both inside and outside Jerusalem.

Having recognized that he lived in a stratified society where oppression was rampant, control being the priority of the scribes, Pharisees, and Sadducees, Jesus chose to not fit into the system. He elected instead to work from the bottom up; hence the controllers of stratification were threatened radically and so felt obliged to destroy him. He made clear that he rejected stratification; that his mission was to ensure that each individual person claimed the dignity that God had freely bestowed on him or her; and that as sons and daughters of God they had a right to live holistically in a liberated, caring, and compassionate society.

The guilty woman was brought to him in the Temple by those who fostered stratification and who strongly opposed the compassionate radicalism of Jesus. They claimed that they wanted him as a teacher of the Law to pass judgment on her. She stood there silent and shivering with fear. She did not dare to speak in the presence of these self-styled eminent scholars. Jesus remained composed and seated.

If he refused to condemn her, he would be accused of rejecting the law of Moses; and if he confirmed that she should be stoned, in keeping with the Law, his adversaries would charge him with disloyalty to Rome since as indicated in John 18:31, Rome had forbidden the Jews to carry out the death penalty as prescribed by their Law.[19] The scene was electric and the tension as they awaited judgment from Jesus was almost unbearable. However, he had wisdom and insight greater than theirs. Without addressing the woman in their presence or questioning the Law, Jesus forced them to pass judgment on themselves and only after they had left the Temple did he communicate directly with the woman. His "judgment" was not a denunciation of the woman. It was rather an invitation to a new and sin-free life. It was a moment of grace and an opportunity for transformation and growth. They had entered the Temple determined to ensnare Jesus and to inflict pain on him and on the defenseless woman. They left condemned by their own conscience, angry and burdened.

Adultery was a sin for which the punishment was death by stoning for both participants (Deut 22:23–24). The nameless woman's accusers knew the Law and could have approached the appropriate authority if they genuinely felt that the ritual had to be observed. Instead they chose to try to trap Jesus. They also chose to ignore their own double standards when dealing with women and men. "The wife and her partner could violate the rights of her husband, but the wife had no rights which her husband could violate."[20] Such a sexual relationship was not adultery if the woman was unmarried. This woman was married. In this case, both participants were guilty. The sin was a shared act, but in this case no retribution was required from the man by this group of legislators. He was allowed to walk free. Pleasure was his prerogative. Punishment was to be the payment for his female partner. Her crime was that she had allowed him to use her body to gratify his carnal desires.

There appears to have been neither discussion nor query as to whether this women was in a free, forced or, as some scholars wonder, an orchestrated situation.[21] The objective of her accusers was not to secure justice, or to reverence the Law, but to entrap Jesus. The woman was simply a tool to help them achieve their purpose. In light of this, it is clear that Jesus was constantly on trial and that his compassion to women, who because of their gender had no rights, was an ideal target. His adversaries were just not going to allow him freedom to minister to the vulnerable unless he adhered to their harsh and unbending rules.

While throughout the gospels Jesus is presented as a faithful Jew, he is also portrayed as one whose liberal and compassionate interpretation of the Law put him at variance with his fellow teachers. He decoded the Law as one who was grounded in mercy, compassion, and life-giving love. He did not make light of sin, as is clear in his brief conversation with the woman following the exit of her accusers. He did not condemn her, but he did direct her not to sin again. That Jesus was unquestionably adverse to the sin of adultery is very clear from his instruction to her and from his teaching on the sanctity of marriage and the destruction brought about by sin throughout the synoptic gospels and especially in Matthew (5:27–32; 15:18–19; 19:18). His acquittal of the woman was in harmony with his mission to save sinners and to empower them to become new participants in the kingdom.

The violence that would have been imparted to the woman would now be directed at Jesus. "By refusing to punish her, he had gathered her guilt to himself. The sin is no less sin for having its sentence commuted; it will still have consequences."[22] It is Jesus who, even at the moment of acquittal, bore these consequences and who would, in a twisted way, be forced by some of the woman's accusers among others to account to the Sanhedrin, Pilate, and Herod for his ministry of compassion in the not-too-distant future.

It is significant that the author of this narrative in John's Gospel tells his readers that Jesus had entered the Temple, the Jewish holy place, from the Mount of Olives. He had been at prayer there immediately before going to teach in the Temple where the woman was presented to him. It would be at the Mount of Olives that Jesus would be arrested after he had shared his Passover meal with the disciples and from where he would be led out to face two trumped-up trials followed by crucifixion on Calvary. In the long term, the scribes, Pharisees, and Sadducees would triumph.

The Temple was the sanctuary of God. It was the holy place about which Ezekiel wrote in terms of the glory of God having been exiled from Jerusalem, only to be returned and restored later. It had returned now in Jesus as mercy, forgiveness, compassion, love, and healing. The Law, its interpretation, and atonement for sins were to be interpreted anew. Love, mercy, and compassion were to be the yardsticks. The true interpretation of the Mosaic Law was to be that God always writes twice (Jn 8:6; 8:8) before passing judgment. In between the "two givings" of the Covenant in the Old Testament, we find the revelation of a forgiving and compassionate God—one who gives a second chance. In commenting on the plight of the woman taken in adultery, Saint Augustine points out that after all had gone away there were only two left: mercy and misery—Jesus and the woman.

God's judgment is salvation—not condemnation.[23] In his directive to the woman that she must not sin again, Jesus offered her the gift of new life and a fresh beginning. She had been transformed and she left a free woman. He, on the other hand, would have to bear the consequences of his actions. As he did this in the Garden, during his trial, and as he struggled to Calvary and died on the cross, is it not reasonable to conclude that this daughter of Jerusalem stood among those women who reached out to him in gratitude, love, and empathy? (Lk 23:27).

Reflection

This story leaves its readers feeling grateful to Jesus, relieved for the woman, and with a number of moral questions regarding the role of the scribes and Pharisees. They said that the woman was "caught in the act of adultery." These were men who were supposed to be paragons of virtue and holiness. If this was a genuine case, how would they have discovered it, or how would they have known where such an illicit relationship was going to be conducted at a time convenient to them? After all, they would have been so busy ensuring their own

29

virtue and the morality of their households that they would not have had time to prowl around the seedy establishments of Jerusalem.

The Mosaic Law clearly laid down that adultery was punishable by stoning to death. Both parties were to be stoned, and not just the woman, as was the case here (Deut 17:5–6; 22:23–24). Furthermore, this penalty was not in use at the time that they were calling for it. Their right to kill had been overruled by the Roman emperor and they knew that Jesus knew that. In addition to this, if the case were to be considered as one that merited stoning, a panel of rabbis, and not just one, as in the case of Jesus, would have had to deal with it. Jesus knew that the scribes and the Pharisees recognized neither him nor his teaching. He also knew that it was not adultery with which they were concerned; rather they sought to discredit him and collect enough evidence to have him condemned.

By taking two periods of time to write on the ground, Jesus gave himself space for discernment. Having been enlightened, he found that he did not need to answer their question. Instead, he challenged them to examine their own conscience and gracefully avoided ensnarement. He forced them to name and to claim their own guilt. He refused to deal with the woman as an object or an abstraction. Instead, he recognized her humanity and placed her on an equal footing with her accusers when he prescribed that the one who was without sin should cast the first stone. Jesus was not concerned with litigation or its theories. His only interest was the human person, and he demanded that each person present examine his own conscience first before passing judgment on any other. That would have included passing judgment on him. He knew, only too well, that they had not gathered to punish an adulteress whether or not she was guilty. They were assembled to condemn him and wished him to do so out of his own mouth.

Having gotten rid of his accusers, Jesus addressed the woman and made clear to her that it was not his mission to condemn. He wanted to give each person a second chance and the advice that would help them to reclaim and then retain their dignity as individuals and as children of a loving God. Jesus' few well-chosen words with the woman seem to indicate that she was guilty. However, there is no way of knowing how or why she came to be in such a relationship. Perhaps she was a prostitute—a woman who would have been ostracized and treated with contempt. If this was the case, it is probable that she was a "working girl" out of necessity and so had a very poor self-image. Jesus restored her dignity. He allowed her to speak for herself and then sent her away with a new vision for her future life. Like so many women in the gospels, she came before him as a victim and left as a liberated woman, who, having been treated with respect, would now be in a position to claim her dignity as a daughter of God.

Presenting her to Jesus for judgment was not a genuine act of virtue. Her litigants had an ulterior motive—to destroy Jesus. That she was a sinner was true. That repentance and atonement on her part were as necessary for her as they are for us today is also true.

- ✺ Are there times in our lives when we connive to destroy others while pretending that we are trying to help them or even save them from some dreadful mistake? Do we sometimes pretend to love tenderly, to act justly, and to walk humbly before our God when in reality we are deceitful and prejudiced power seekers whose real aim in life is self-advancement, self-gratification, and control of others?

- ✺ As we proceed on our Lenten pilgrimage and look back at our lives with a view to renewal and transformation, can we identify times when we have positively set ourselves the task of preventing others in our local community or workplace from being as effective as they could be had we not prevented their progress? Have there been times when we have purposely excluded others from a group activity or exercise out of jealousy, self-interest, or because of our own insecurity?

❧ It is possible that the scribes and the Pharisees orchestrated the situation with the woman regardless of her occupation or marital fidelity. In our relationships and employment or ministry, have we ever compromised others in order to advance ourselves or to restrict their opportunities? Do we sometimes use body language with the intention of confusing, diverting, or deceiving in order to score points, to marginalize others, or to limit their freedom? Where do we stand on justice issues? Are we armchair critics, or do we speak out even if we risk being victimized ourselves?

The drama in the case of the woman caught in the act of adultery became quiet and the suspense deepened when Jesus took time to bend down from his seat and write in the dust. It reached an unexpected conclusion when he looked up and challenged them in a way that gave the woman a second chance through forcing her accusers to confront their own demons.

❧ In unpleasant situations where we have to pass judgments and make difficult decisions, are we agents of tranquillity in an effort to ensure justice through careful discernment, or do we rush into making judgments that may be political but result in the poor and vulnerable being oppressed or marginalized?

❧ If we hold positions of leadership, do we try to mirror God by writing twice in the dust in order to reveal to those who underachieve or appear to fail us, their own potential and their right to a second chance? On the other hand, are we so terrorized by the scribes and Pharisees of our day—the media and the economy of success—that we always feel obliged to pass ill-informed and detrimental judgments?

A compassionate look, word, or act from Jesus empowered women and changed the course of their lives. Without having had an encounter with him, how oppressed and restricted would many of them have been? If we genuinely want to embrace the gospel this Lent, we must allow ourselves to take time to bend down and "write on the ground" before we look up to deliver a judgment. Otherwise, we may find that on Easter Sunday while others, staying close to the ground, are looking up at God and singing alleluias, we ourselves are in self-enforced silence and condemned to looking at the ground from a self-constructed Calvary.

The Unnamed Samaritan Woman

JOHN 4:7–38
MARK 15:40

THIS WOMAN REPRESENTS all unnamed women who were ministered to by Jesus on his way from Galilee through Samaria and into Jerusalem at various times. She also represents all those who, like Pilate's wife, came from outside Judaism and who were drawn to him by faith. Such women are accounted for by Luke as *"women who bewailed and lamented him"* (23:27).

> *So he came to a city of Samar'ia, called Sy'char, near the field that Jacob gave to his son Joseph. Jacob's well was there, and so Jesus, wearied as he was with his journey, sat down beside the well. It was about the sixth hour. There came a woman of Samar'ia to draw water. Jesus said to her, "Give me a drink"* (Jn 4:5–7).

John has placed this woman's story at a very significant point in his gospel. Jesus has only recently been ostracized by his own people, the

34

Jews, during his cleansing of the Temple (Jn 2:13–25). In a very short space of time, after that painful incident, John has him traveling from Galilee through Samaria on his way back to Jerusalem, and engaged in conversation with a self-composed Samaritan woman who, like himself, has been ostracized by her own people. He is resting as he returns to the city that has no room for him and that will eventually vote that he should be crucified (Mt 27:23). In contrast to his own people, this well-informed Samaritan housewife has accepted his invitation to engage in conversation. She challenges, questions, and is transformed as a result of his communication with her.

She had been going about her daily business. She had a home and a partner to care for and, however others may have viewed her domestic situation, she was happy in it at that moment in time. Like every other female who has lived into womanhood, she was carrying a certain amount of painful baggage, which she wished to preserve as her private business. But clearly she had been unsuccessful as is obvious from the fact that she was alone at the well at a time when all the other women had either already drawn their water for the day or would do so later in the evening at around dusk. Like Jesus, she was an outcast. She had been ostracized by her community because of her unconventional lifestyle. As she made clear in her communication with Jesus, she was conscious of her current spiritual and moral status.

She knew the teaching of the Pentateuch and the promise of the Messiah, but she had been unlucky in love and had chosen to live a life that caused her to be rejected as an outcast. She was aware of how Jews viewed Samaritans and did not seek to hide this knowledge: *"How is it that you, a Jew, ask a drink of me, a woman of Samar'ia?"* (Jn 4:9). A lone female, she was seeking neither conversation nor conversion from a member of a race who considered themselves superior to hers. The fact that she is the only person in the gospels to refer to Jesus as "a Jew" demonstrates that she had her own thoughts about Jews and did not hide her astonishment that he had approached her.

However, her curiosity got the better of her and since he initiated a conversation, she took time to engage with him. After all, she was experienced in talking with men. The dialogue led from the concrete water that would quench bodily thirst, to the spiritual and theological, which would lead to eternal life. She quickly discovered that this man was different from those with whom she had previously related. He was more interested in what was hidden in the depth of her soul than what was openly on display. He neither affirmed her in her lifestyle nor pretended to be ignorant of her circumstances. "He encountered her precisely at the point of her own self-inflicted brokenness, which, paradoxically, served as her claim to righteousness. She gave him her poverty when she confessed her sin."[24] Jesus challenged her in that poverty and transformed her spiritually and emotionally. A woman of the dark, she had come to the well at noon, the height of sunlight. Through her conversation with Jesus she put the darkness of sin behind her and became a daughter of the light. Just as the male disciples had left their nets on the seashore at Galilee (Jn 1:40–41), now she left her water vessel and hurried like Andrew to spread the good news and to extend the discipleship (Jn 4:28a).

Just then his disciples came. They marveled that he was talking with a woman, but none said, "What do you wish?" or, "Why are you talking with her?" (Jn 4:27)

This gave Jesus an opportunity to engage with them in a session of catechesis (4:31–38). They were still controlled by the Jewish narrow-minded interpretation of the Law and its dictates on purity observances and intergender communications. While Jesus understood their reaction, it pained him. However, he did not display any emotion, but focused instead on his and their ongoing work of evangelization. Every thought, word, and action must be focused on the kingdom.

Meanwhile the Samaritan woman was so astounded by what Jesus told her that she left her water jar and went to call her neighbors to him.

> *"Come, see a man who told me all that I ever did. Can this be the Christ?"…Many Samaritans from that city believed in him because of the woman's testimony…* (Jn 4:29, 39).

She had set out on a journey at midday with one mission in mind, but she returned home in the afternoon having abandoned it in favor of a greater one. She had understood and accepted the symbolism of the water and through it brought her local community to faith. "Among the fundamental values linked to women's actual lives is what has been called a capacity for the other."[25] Here was a woman who exhibited that value at its best. In this woman Scripture gives us a portrait of the first true missionary. She represents all that the gospel is about,[26] and she is a symbol of all faith-filled women. It is most likely that she was one of the women described by Mark as *"looking on from afar"* (15:40) as Jesus labored toward Calvary. "She is a summary of how people come to understand Jesus: first as a Jew; then as a prophet; then as the Messiah; then as the Saviour of the world."[27]

Reflection

In this story Jesus was away from his disciples. He was tired, weary, and thirsty. But still he was on his mission. Unlike the Wayne Rooneys, Tom Cruises, or Simon Cowells or indeed any of the media-conscious politicians of our day, he had no press or media following noting his every movement. This did not bother him because he was about his *"Father's house"* (Lk 2:49).

The woman came looking for water to enable her to provide temporal nourishment for her household. Like so many of us who go shopping for one thing and end up purchasing something totally different, she arrived knowing what she wanted but returned with something totally different. She had had a life-changing experience. She had been warmly greeted by a foreigner who treated her with respect and engaged her in conversation. He had not lectured her on morality or sin. He had rather challenged and energized her. She had found faith, made a friend, and was the bearer of news to her neighborhood that brought them out to meet a new hero (Jn 4:39).

- During our "forty days in the desert," are there lessons we might learn from this Samaritan woman's story? Where do we stand in relation to ethnicity and cross-cultural relationships? Are there people in our neighborhood or parish whom we would term "foreigners," "unclean," "amoral," or beneath us?

- Are we willing to entertain and share with refugees, or do we see them as freeloaders who unjustly make claims on the health and welfare and Social Security services and avail themselves of charity or take jobs that we consider the prerogative of "our people"?

- Do we make the vulnerable suffer today, as the disciples contributed to Jesus' sufferings, because of our own legalism in terms of the sacraments, our self-righteousness, and our skepticism about their motives and actions? Do we rashly judge and ill treat those who do not fit into the mold that we have shaped for them? Do we try to imprison others by excluding them from ministry so that we can be in control?

≈ Are we, like the disciples, critical in our hearts or do we gossip about our parish team and council members, instead of voicing our concerns in the right place; or are we, like the Woman at the Well, ready to leave our egocentricity behind us in order to be available for ministry?

Possibly, we are already conscious that nobody goes through life without entering Samaria at some point. It is not just entering Samaria that touches our lives. It is, rather, what we do while there that is important and how we allow our experiences to shape our lives. The disciples of Jesus saw Samaria as a place to be avoided and to be left behind as quickly as possible. Jesus, on the other hand, saw it as fertile ground crying out for evangelization. He pleaded with the disciples to look around them and see how ripe the "crops" were. He urged them to slow down and prepare to save a rich harvest for their God.

No one in the Christian Church today can deny that its members are not in a type of Samaria. For years we have been plagued with scandals and accusations of child sex abuse that have rocked the foundations of our Church. The impression has been given in certain media circles that secrecy, sexual impropriety, pedophilia, abuse of women in general and of consecrated women in particular, and corruption abound. This has had an adverse effect on vocations to the consecrated life and to the ordained ministry and particularly so in the Roman Catholic Church in the West where celibacy is still mandatory. However, there are still thousands of wonderful young people out there who have looked around them and seen the potential that exists for revitalization and transformation. They crave to be involved if only we will create space for them.

≈ Do we realize that we need to pray for the grace to allow young people space and freedom in the vineyard?

When Jesus pointed out the potential in Samaria to the disciples, *"I tell you, lift up your eyes, and see how the fields are already white for harvest"* (Jn 4:35), he was referring to the interest that the Samaritan woman had aroused in her people. Furthermore, he was encouraging them to put their prejudices aside, to be holistic in their vision, and to embrace diversity for the sake of the kingdom. Today he is calling parents in general and women in particular to awaken their children to the need for evangelizers.

❦ Do we accept that if our parishes are to have pastors in the future we will have to provide them from our own offspring?

This Lent let each of us mothers, teachers, and pastors make it our special mission, in reading the signs of the times, to join the Samaritan woman in calling the attention of our sons and daughters to *"the fields that are already white with harvest"* in today's Samaria.

The Named Women Who Traveled From Galilee With Jesus

MARK 15:40

There were also women looking on from afar, among whom were Mary Mag'dalene, and Mary the mother of James the younger and of Joses, and Salo'me, who, when he was in Galilee, followed him, and ministered to him (Mk 15:40–41a).

HERE THE GOSPELS introduce us to another group of named and unnamed women who, with Mary the mother of Jesus, would have been leaders in the infant church. During our Lenten meditations these women may speak in a special way to those of us women who hold positions of responsibility in the Christian community or who serve in the consecrated life. They had been in discipleship with Jesus throughout his ministry, and with their leader, Mary Magdalene, made their own contribution. We know this because when we study the lists provided by the three evangelists who give names, and allow for divergence, we notice that a total of five are identified as having independent status. That some evangelists name some women and not others is agreed by scholars as to be expected since there was a tendency to simply name those women with whom readers were familiar or those who had already been identified in the oral tradition.[28] In our consideration of the unnamed members, we shall reflect on the stories of two who would have had personal and missionary reasons to be present for Jesus. The Scripture texts listing the named women are as follows:

- Matthew 27:56: *"Mary Magdalene, and Mary the mother of James and Joseph, and the mother of the sons of Zebedee— [Salome]."*

- Mark 15:40: *"...among whom were Mary Magdalene, and Mary the mother of James the younger and of Joses, and Salo'me."*

- John 19:25: *"Standing by the cross of Jesus were his mother, and his mother's sister, Mary the wife of Clopas, and Mary Magdalene."*

The presence of these brave and faithful women stands in sharp contrast to their male counterparts. Only John is mentioned in one gospel as having been on Calvary with Jesus and for Mary his mother. In the resurrection narratives it is to the women that Jesus showed himself first (Mt 28:9; Mk 16:9; Jn 20:13). They, too, were the initial group to be commissioned as witnesses to the resurrection (Mt 28:10; Mk 16:7,10, Jn 20:16, 17). From this it is clear that Jesus rewarded fidelity and saw women taking a leading role in ministry as the first witnesses in partnership with Peter and the other disciples.

In commenting on the role of women in Jesus' ministry, Edith Dean writes, "Evidently Matthew believes that women are guarantors of the tradition."[29] This is a powerful thought and a huge challenge to women, to the men in ordained ministry, and above all to the magisterium in this third millennium when there is almost a crisis in terms of faith in the Western Church and a huge shortage of sacramental ministers.

Mary Magdalene

MATTHEW 27:56
MARK 15:40
JOHN 19:25

WE SHALL NOW REFLECT BRIEFLY briefly on each of the named women in the group who traveled with Jesus from Galilee. Many modern scholars see Mary Magdalene as having as significant a ministry as Peter during Jesus' ministry, albeit in different ways.[30]

Jesus said to her, "Mary." She turned and said to him in Hebrew, "Rab-bo'ni!" (which means Teacher) (Jn 20:16).

Excluding his mother, the leading disciple, and the one who appears to have been closest to Jesus not just during his ministry but on the cross, too, was Mary Magdalene. The fact that she was free to follow Jesus consistently indicates that she was a single woman who had few home duties and that she was of comfortable means. Many scholars believe that, like Joanna (Lk 8:3; 24:10), Mary put her resources at the service of Jesus and his disciples' ministry. In her time Magdala was a thriving and popular town, and a center for commercial sexual activity at the south of the plain of Gennesaret.

Scholars emphasize that this Mary is not to be confused with Mary of Bethany, who anointed Jesus' head in anticipation of his impending passion, death, and rushed burial.[31] They are two separate characters, each identified by the name of the town where she resided. Mary's name occurs on fourteen occasions in the Gospels—considerably more frequently than any other female disciple, even Jesus' mother. In eight of the passages she heads the list of women disciples, in one she is second only to Jesus' mother, and in five she appears alone.[32] This is ample evidence that she held the leadership among the women and that she was totally and unconditionally committed to Jesus' ministry and mission.

It is widely believed that she is the woman whom Jesus healed from grave illness. We read in Mark's Gospel:

When he rose early on the first day of the week, he appeared first to Mary Magdalene, from whom he had cast out seven demons (Mk 16:9; Lk 8:2).

However, it would be unfair to take this sentence literally. To the Jews, seven was a complete or mystic number. It occurs 465 times in the Bible, and 318 of these occurrences are in the Old Testament. Scholars suggest that rather than having been possessed by demons, Mary suffered from a nervous disorder—possibly epilepsy. Whatever her illness, it is clear that Jesus healed her and that in gratitude she became one of his greatest converts and most loyal supporters. Herbert Lockyer and others argue that a careful reading of the gospels portrays her as a pure, caring, committed, trusted, loyal, and faithful disciple.

To suggest that she was dissolute because she was possessed by seven devils, is to affirm that every insane person is depraved. There is no word whatever in the writings of the Christian Fathers, whose authority stands next to the apostles, as to Mary having a foul reputation.[33]

The misconception about her lack of purity in her earlier life may have arisen because Luke places the story of the healing of the woman who was a sinner immediately before he accounts for the women who were followers of Jesus (Lk 8:36–50). Hers is one of many stories in the New Testament that illustrate the level of Jesus' success in healing and in restoring people to dignity through his outreach in mercy. "People move from the marginalized fringes to prominence as examples worthy of praise and emulation because of their encounters and their response to Jesus."[34] A careful study of Scripture shows Mary Magdalene to be a woman of exemplary character, courage, mercy, faith, and unswerving fidelity. The fact that three of the four evangelists make so much of her position on Calvary and that John singles her out from all those women who rushed to the tomb on Easter day illustrates the quality of her virtue and the important leadership role that she exercised among the women disciples.

Three of the gospels speak of the nervous, frightened group of women who stood at a distance from the cross of Jesus. John has Mary Magdalene in there in the thick of the action with Jesus' mother and her sister-in-law. She was a risk taker and a woman of mercy, and in mercy she fearlessly stood at the foot of the cross. At a spiritual level it was her cross too, and she demonstrated that by her closeness to Jesus. The depth of her sorrow and, at the same time, the level of affirmation, consolation, mercy, and love that she extended to him must have left her feeling drained and exhausted. In a clear demonstration that Jesus' relationship with Mary Magdalene was spiritual, mission centered, and platonic, he did not utter any special concern for her. Suffering was part of his ministry and it would continue to be so for Mary and all those devoted women who followed her example in discipleship. Jesus singled out his mother alone as special and in need of protection.

Mary Magdalene's selflessness and humility are demonstrated again by the fact that she did not resent Jesus' acknowledgment of his mother and his apparent blindness to her presence. She was there in the ministry of mercy, and all she wanted was to support. Bravely, and in silence, she watched him die. With John and his aunt, she comforted his mother as he was lifted down from the cross. Then, conscious of the haste in which he had been killed, and the need for a quick burial, she realized that the traditional embalming rituals could not be carried out and that it would be necessary to observe them later. She reverently followed the cortege to the garden tomb and took special note of the burial place so that she, with the other women disciples, could return and carry out the final rituals after the Sabbath.

Mary is the steadfast one of the New Testament, the one who loved unconditionally and with an unceasing intensity. She openly identified with Jesus in good times and in bad times, in moments of joy and celebration; and she was there with equal involvement in moments of apparent despair. She is the one female disciple whose ministry and role in leadership has been diminished in the minds of Christians because of the androcentric influences of those who were the final editors of the Good News and their need to emphasize the role of Peter as Jesus' successor. She stands in sharp contrast to him on Calvary and again on Easter morning when she had to call him to go to the tomb. She, not Peter or John, provides continuity from Galilee to Jerusalem, from Jerusalem to Calvary, from Calvary to the tomb, and from the tomb to a resurrected and glorified figure in the garden (Jn 20:16b).

Reflection

Mary Magdalene presents each of us with a huge challenge in terms of courage, mercy, availability, generosity, and steadfastness in ministry. Her example of unconditional loyalty and fidelity invites each of us to reflect on our prayer life, purity of intention, and faithfulness to our commitment in life—be that to marriage, celibacy in the single state, or in the consecrated life.

- Are we givers in terms of time and the few resources of which we have some degree of personal ownership, or are we selective about our availability and hoarders of our possessions?

- Do we put people and their worthiness of our ministry into categories according to what we think of their current social standing? Are we seekers and doers, or are we selfish when it comes to being there for one another and for those who do not appear to us to deserve either our presence or our service? When those who live closest to us meet us, do they recognize us as apostles of the Good News of a risen Christ or are they transported instantly to the cross?

- Are we willing to risk unpopularity with local government leaders, policymakers, and the so-called wealthy in an effort to secure justice or mercy for victims of racism, social or consecrated discrimination, abusive relationships, or any of the many forms of addiction that destroy their dignity as children of God?

- Mary used her resources to serve the needs of her day and her ministry. Where do we stand on issues of our day—the environment, the abuse of the natural resources of our earth, and pollution of minds, hearts, and the environment?

Mary was an Easter woman: "Alleluia" was her song. Let's join her with renewed enthusiasm this Lent and passiontide in bringing the good news to "today's Peter," even if (s)he only lives or works next door. If our intentions in ministry at home and in our locality are as pure as Mary's were, the Peter at the end of the street or in the next parish will be helped to say "Rab-bo'ni!" by a new Mary Magdalene this Eastertide.

Mary the Mother of James and Joses

MARK 15:40

YET ANOTHER MARY stood by Jesus to the end.

There were also women looking on from afar, among whom were Mary Mag'dalene, and Mary the mother of James the younger and of Joses... (Mk 15:40).

The names James and Joses first appear in Mark 6:3, at a time when the authority of Jesus is first questioned in public. The Mary referred to then, and now, at the cross creates an ambiguity for all who study and reflect on the Word of God. Some scholars suggest that this is most probably Mary the mother of Jesus. Catholic academics hold that the relationship of the two men to Mary is indeed a blood relationship and that she is their mother, but add that she is not the mother of Jesus. She was, they believe, another aunt to Jesus. John's account of the crucifixion would support this view because he actually names the Mary at the foot of the cross as Jesus' mother and he makes no reference to James and Joses. To follow Mark's suggestion literally is to place Mary the mother of Jesus with the other women at a distance from the cross. Scholars hold that it is most unlikely that Jesus' mother would have selected a safe space for herself and taken a position at a distance from him in his hour of greatest need.

While it has to be recognized that, to date, researchers do not seem to have retrieved any detail on the life of Mary the mother of James and Joses, many accept that she is indeed a separate person and that it can be taken for granted that Mary of Nazareth was with her son on his way to Calvary, and that she remained close to him on his cross, even if Mark never mentioned the fact.

Scholars continue to wrestle with this ambiguity. Some Protestant theologians seem to exclude Mary the mother of James and Joses from the cross and to explain by stating that the Mary referred to here is Mary the mother of Jesus, who had other biological children. Catholic scholars, on the other hand, state that Mary the mother of James and Joses was at the cross as Jesus' aunt, and that she is identified through her sons because they were disciples of Jesus who would have been remembered by the communities who were being addressed by Matthew and Mark.

Scholars believe that like the mother of the sons of Zebedee, Mary the mother of James and Joses was a widow, or that she was the wife of a man who was possibly not a member of the faith community. Had her husband been alive or a known member of the discipleship, she would have been identified through him rather than through her sons. Mark makes clear that she was certainly the mother of the disciple James—sometimes called "the less" or "the younger" to distinguish him from the more prominent disciple, James the brother of John (Mk 15:40). It would appear that Joses came to faith later than his brother and that if he had a definite discipleship role before Jesus' passion, it may have been as one of the seventy-two or as part of some other small-team partnership in ministry.

In commenting on this Mary, the Protestant scholar, Herbert Lockyer writes,

We do know that she was one of the women who followed Jesus, and having sufficient wealth, ministered unto Him and His disciples in material things thereby assisting them in their work.[35]

In support of this assertion, he used Luke 8:2–3: *"And the twelve were with him, and also some women who had been healed of evil spirits and infirmities."* He also believes that Mary's sons were older than Jesus as they were among the group of family who tried to reason with him when concern grew about his workload in the early days of his ministry (Mk 3:21). If Lockyer is right in his reasoning, it is likely that Mary was one of those who had received a healing from Jesus and through it had found faith. She nurtured this faith and not only sacrificed her sons to its service but gave of her own physical, spiritual, and material resources as well.

She is named as one of those who rushed to the tomb on Easter day with spices to anoint the body of Jesus. Hers would have been a simple and pious faith. For that reason, she is a model for many mothers and grandmothers who feel indebted to Divine Providence for the many graces received in their own and in their children's lives. She presents a challenge to all parents who actively seek to prevent their children from becoming full-time partners in spreading the good news and in ministering to God's people. This Mary would not have been one for solo trips, prominence, or position. She was a team person, and it was as a member of a team that her fidelity, faith, generosity, and simplicity were rewarded when she received word that Jesus had conquered death and sin forever.

Reflection

This Mary is a model of generosity, selflessness, bravery, and graciousness. She is a woman who successfully brought up good sons and supported them in both their faith commitment and in their ministry. As a widow, she would have had a right to expect at least one of her boys to stay at home and continue the family fishing business with her. Not only did she give them total freedom in choosing how they used their gifts, but she also joined them in ministry.

She is an excellent role model for young widows and for single mothers who have raised families and are young enough to think of giving themselves in full-time ministry to the Church. She had done her life's work and had every reason to sit back and enjoy a well-deserved retirement. However, she was too selfless, noble, and generous to contemplate such a lifestyle. She had lived for her boys, and she would continue to be there for them and for their partners in ministry. The ministry of Jesus needed to be carried forward, and Mary, being a follower rather than a leader, chose to make her contribution by joining the existing discipleship rather than by creating a new fellowship, which while it might have been good in itself, could have simply resulted in a duplication of objectives. Such an action could have resulted in retrenchment rather than the expansion of the mission.

- ❧ When we reflect on our own time in life, on the needs of our local community, and on the needs of the Church for more women to give themselves to part- or full-time ministry, how do we react?

- ❧ Do we sit back and tell ourselves that we have done our bit and that it is time for others to make a contribution, or do we approach a charitable organization, church group, consecrated congregation, or other group in ministry and offer to make ourselves and/or our resources available for the spread of the good news?

Jesus never made age a barrier to ministry and we would do well to follow his example. Only two of his disciples are thought to have been in what might be called the younger age bracket—James the younger and the Beloved Disciple. All the women in ministry seem to have been of mature years. Jesus called all ages during his ministry, and he continues to issue the same call and invitation today.

❧ Are we listening and, if we are, are we allowing ourselves to hear his invitation? We do not need to take on the world on our own.

During this Lent, let us remember to pray that today's women will be open to the Holy Spirit at work in their lives. Let us ask that through the intercession of Mary the mother of James and Joses, widows and single mothers may be particularly alert to the Church's need for their special contribution to the mission of Jesus.

❧ If we are widowed and retired from paid employment, are there activities in our parish in which we could usefully be engaged, such as visiting the sick, elderly, prisoners, helping the homeless, supporting literacy programs, or maybe offering ourselves in the consecrated life?

Salome

MARK 15:40

SALOME IS MENTIONED in the list with Mary Magdalene:

…among whom were Mary Mag'dalene, and Mary the mother of James the younger and of Joses, and Salo'me (Mark 15:40).

Salome was an inhabitant of Capernaum, on the Sea of Galilee. She was probably the mother of the sons of Zebedee (some scholars debate this point).[36] She would have been known to Jesus from the very early days of his ministry, having been the mother of two of his first disciples. She is best remembered as the one who tried to influence him into allocating special positions for her sons (Mt 20:21). Being human and ambitious for her boys, she was presumptuous enough to put her desire for prestigious positions before the spiritual formation, character building, and ministry of her sons.[37] In doing this, she simply demonstrated that she was a typical mother. She is the one with whom all determined mothers down through history have been able to identify and from whom they have, in terms of a sound spirituality of mercy, been able to learn the authentic definition of true greatness in times of prayer and reflection.

Her request gave Jesus an opportunity to deliver one of his finest teachings of true greatness (Mt 20:26). She did not succeed with her petition, and she was sensible enough not to let the fact that she failed to achieve her ambition adversely affect her relationship with Jesus. He would have been a frequent visitor to her home and she probably viewed him as one of the family. She was probably older than Mary Magdalene, Mary the wife of Clopas, Mary the mother of Jesus, and Mary the mother of James and Joses. However, it is not thought that she was considered the leader of the group of women. Scholars believe that was the prerogative of Mary Magdalene, a single woman who was in full-time ministry.

Salome ran a household and had too many responsibilities in the domestic ministry of the entire discipleship to be the vision creator for the holy women. She was probably the trusted older woman, who held a consultative and supporting role, and who was available to travel with them when they really needed her unique skills. She was a model of fidelity, one who was admired and respected by all. She is named by Matthew and Mark as one of those who stood at the foot of the cross after having made that painful journey from Jerusalem. Furthermore, she is identified by Mark as having been the companion to Mary Magdalene, who prepared the spices and rushed to the tomb on Easter day to anoint the body of Jesus.

She is seen as a key participant in the entire Jesus story because she is named third in Mark's list of those women who witnessed the death of Jesus, the place where he was buried, and because she went with Mary Magdalene and Mary the mother of James to the tomb on Easter day (Mk 15:40, 47; 16:1). However, it is for her presence on Calvary that she is most frequently remembered by mothers who suffer with their children. With the other women she was consumed by love and sympathy. With a painful heart she stood bravely near the cross in an effort to be a source of consolation and affirmation to the one she had grown to love as a son and as the Messiah.

Reflection

Salome was a blunt and straightforward woman who did not believe in beating about the bush as far as her sons were concerned. She knew what she wanted and made her desire known directly to Jesus. Her evangelization was not yet complete. She was a woman of means and like many mothers, she wanted a status for her sons that would be a considerable improvement on that enjoyed by their father, who had worked hard all his years to secure the best for his boys and their mother.

Because she had struggled to achieve the social position that she currently occupied in the local fishing community she could not think beyond the material. She had not gotten the message that the ministry about which Jesus spoke had nothing to do with social position, earthly power, or financial status. It was about love, mercy, and justice for people of all ages, places, and occupations. It was about equality in community. Jesus' ministry was about service—a work that was then, in Judaism, and still is in the Church today—seen as the occupation of women and something that goes unacknowledged or is merely patronized.

- ✇ Are we aware that our own evangelization is an ongoing process and that Lent is a special time when the Church presents us with opportunities to deepen our faith and to share it with others in a mutually enriching way?

- ✇ Where do we stand in relation to ministry, and are we willing to serve others regardless of their apparent ingratitude or unworthiness?

If we see it as a symbol of status, we are not in ministry. We are rather on an ego trip and our achievements, however great they may appear to us, will die with us. Jesus spoke frankly to Salome when she showed that she was still functioning at a pre- or early-catechumenate level. She had only had a short time of working in partnership with Jesus and could be forgiven for her misunderstanding. Each of us has had considerably longer, and we have had many more opportunities to immerse ourselves in the teaching of Jesus. We know the corporal works of mercy, and we have had the experience of receiving their fruits from members of our Christian community on numerous occasions. We have little excuse for living and thinking like those who have not yet been through a grounded process of evangelization.

- Where are we when it comes to positions of power?

- Do we neglect to examine our own conscience and spend time labeling others as power mongers when all the time we are cheating ourselves by hiding behind those we condemn?

- Are we as enthusiastic to ensure that widows, the sons and daughters of refugees, prisoners, and victims of abuse, injustice, and domestic violence are given their rights in justice and mercy, as we are delighted to see honors afforded to those who already hold positions of status in society?

Not until we confront our own demons and admit to our own desire for power can we escape the fatal loop of manipulating others in order to gain "first place." We must remind ourselves frequently that the only first place that really matters here and in eternity is the one allocated to us by the Father, who alone assesses the true worth of our work for that love in mercy that is authentic ministry.

Mary the Wife of Clopas

JOHN 19:25A

JOHN LISTS MARY the wife of Clopas as the second woman who stood at the foot of the cross in support of both Jesus and his mother Mary.

> *[S]tanding by the cross of Jesus were his mother, and his mother's sister, Mary the wife of Clopas...* (Jn 19:25a).

This is the only time that Mary the wife of Clopas is mentioned in the gospels. It is not surprising because, on the whole, women get limited press in the Scriptures and when they are mentioned, it is in terms of their sinfulness, their need of healing, or because they are models of self-sacrifice. Mary the wife of Clopas fits most comfortably into the model of self-sacrificing women. She is portrayed as one who was there for others. She is named second in John's list of women at the cross, and there she is identified as *"his mother's sister"* (Jn 19:25b). It has been accepted generally in some Catholic circles over the years that this Mary, the wife of Clopas, was literally the blood sister of Mary the mother of Jesus. Many scholars today challenge that on the basis that it is most unlikely that two blood sisters would have the same name. Others wonder how it is possible to know anything about someone who has been given such a brief mention in sacred Scripture. But it is on such references that historians depend in their investigations into the lives of some of the most wonderful and inspiring people in the Bible.

Such historical information about people who played a part in the origins of Christianity should not be despised. It is on the accumulation and interpretation of such information that accurate understanding of the early Church as a historical movement depends. In the case of Mary of Clopas, what we can know about her will contribute to our understanding both of the roles that relatives of Jesus played in the early Church and of the roles that women played."[38]

Scholarly research now indicates that Mary the wife of Clopas was, in fact, the sister-in-law to Mary the mother of Jesus. Clopas was the brother of Joseph, who was the husband of Mary. The name Clopas was extremely rare, as Bauckham points out, and historical research indicates strongly that the Clopas of John 19:25 and of Luke 24:18 was indeed the brother of Joseph. This Mary had a very famous son, Simon, who succeeded his cousin James as a leader in the Church in Jerusalem until he was martyred under Trajan (Roman Emperor AD 98–117). "He was the most important Christian leader in Palestine for half a century."[39] If this is the case, first readers of John's Gospel would have had no problem in recognizing Mary of Clopas.

Her presence at the cross would have been as a member of Jesus' family. She would have been there to empathize with Jesus, to affirm his innocence, and to extend love, sympathy, and mercy to his mother. This Mary's faith in Jesus, her commitment to his interpretation of the

Law, and her fidelity in ministry would have encouraged the mother of Jesus and affirmed her belief in his innocence. It would have served to all present as a beacon of hope in what appeared to the male disciples to be a scene of utter disaster.

In researching ministry and mission during Jesus' active ministry, modern biblical scholars point to the importance of small-group and paired partnerships. They derive some of their considerations and claims from Luke as follows:

After this the Lord appointed seventy others, and sent them on ahead of him, two by two, into every town and place where he himself was about to come (Lk 10:1).

Following this model of mission, some scholars suggest that it is quite possible that the two disciples who accompanied Jesus on their way to Emmaus were Mary and Clopas. If this theory is true and, from the evidence available, there is no reason to disbelieve it, it would make sense that having appeared to so many of the disciples on Easter day, Jesus would present himself to Mary and Clopas too, as a reward for their fidelity throughout his public life and particularly during his passion, death on the cross, and support to his mother following his burial.

It is interesting that Jesus was recognized in a situation of ministry and hospitality. Mary and Clopas had prevailed on him to join them for a meal (Lk 24:28–30). They had known the details of Jesus' life and ministry, of his crucifixion, and of his entombment and they needed to unburden the story to their guest. They were mere human beings who had so recently suffered the most cruel and unjust bereavement. They needed to talk it through with an outsider. They needed to process their story as part of accepting it and as part of gaining healing. They were, in all ways, like us. They had a deep need for a listening ear and an understanding heart.

More important, despite all they had been through, they were still believers. With Clopas, Mary was a just woman. She had known Jesus to be a just, merciful, honest, and Spirit-filled man and this knowledge had brought her to an unswerving faith. Her faith was rewarded when he revealed himself to them in the breaking of bread. Luke records the revelation as follows:

When he was at table with them, he took the bread and blessed, and broke it, and gave it to them. And their eyes were opened and they recognized him; and he vanished out of their sight. They said to each other, "Did not our hearts burn within us while he talked to us on the road, while he opened to us the scriptures?" (Lk 24:30–32)

All that she, in her defenselessness, loyalty, and integrity had suffered as she stood with her few female companions by the cross was erased from her memory in an instant and forever. From now on, all she would remember was the joy of recognizing the glorified Jesus and it was this that fueled her and her husband Clopas for ministry in the future.

Reflection

Three of the wonderful characteristics of this Mary that shine out from her one brief mention in Scripture are her steadfastness in times of suffering and apparent disaster; her fearlessness in a situation of political and consecrated bigotry, tension, threat, and real danger; and her integrity in a situation where she was likely to be humiliated and at risk of bringing shame on herself and her family. She was a woman of courage, faith, and honor. She recognized both justice and injustice, and she was determined to prove by her presence at the foot of the cross that she was not afraid of those who were the bedfellows of injustice. She was not afraid of those who only felt safe when they had destroyed the good, the merciful, and the gentle.

She stands out as an inspiration to all women who work for justice through silent protest and by standing up in public for those who are not in a position to defend themselves and their rights.

- ✎ Are we willing to follow her example and to become the silent but public presence of the oppressed, abused, murdered, and disappeared in places such as Northern Ireland, Lebanon, Sudan, Iraq, South Africa, Kosovo, Rwanda, Chile, and in all political and consecrated situations where the bomb, the bullet, the pen, and the gun are used to terrorize and control?

- ✎ What action do we take when we are aware of a culture of cover-up, concealment, and deception against the innocent?

- ✎ Are we active protesters against evil and promoters of justice or just passive observers in situations where women—consecrated and lay—and children are the fertile grounds on which users, abusers, the insecure, and faceless control freaks thrive in both Church and state?

Mary was a woman of mercy, memory, and vision. In our broken world these are virtues that are greatly needed. In our prayer this Lent and passiontide, let us ask Jesus to imbue us with these virtues so that on Easter day we may recognize him holistically in first, the breaking of bread, and second, in all victims of injustice in our community and in the Church, and in all members of our renewed faith community.

The Unnamed Women Who Traveled From Galilee With Jesus

There were also women looking on from afar...and also many other women who came up with him to Jerusalem (Mk 15:40, 41).

IN REFLECTING ON this passage of Scripture we shall consider the stories of two women who, as representatives of all the women who received healing, looked on in empathy as Jesus moved out on the final stage of his torturous journey.

The Woman With the Hemorrhage

MARK 5:25–34
MATTHEW 9:20–22
LUKE 8:43–48

SHE HAD FOLLOWED Jesus toward the house of Jarius when she needed healing and caused his disciples to challenge him when he stopped to demonstrate that he had the power and authority to heal through faith and touch alone. Although the disciples lived closely with him, they were never sure of his identity. This uncertainty would continue and be a source of pain to him throughout his ministry. It would culminate for him and for Peter in the courtyard of Caiaphas (Mk 14:66–72). However, it is reasonable to believe that this "daughter" did know him, and having had her faith transformed, continued to be a witness for Jesus to the end as one of *"the women who had followed him from Galilee, stood at a distance and saw these things"* (Lk 23:49).

"Daughter, your faith has made you well; go in peace, and be healed of your disease" (Mk 5:34).

This was Jesus' response to her faith and to her courage in identifying herself in public after he had healed her.

Mark writes, *"But the woman, knowing what had been done to her, came in fear and trembling and fell down before him, and told him the whole truth"* (Mk 5:33). It was then that Jesus spoke with empathy and compassion to her saying, *"Daughter, your faith has made you well; go in peace, and be healed of your disease"* (Mk 5:34). This woman, like every other woman who approached Jesus in the gospels, displayed great faith and that faith was rewarded, affirmed, enhanced, and brought to the attention of those present. Because of her illness the woman was ostracized by her community as she was said to be unclean under the consecrated implication of the Law. Women were considered unclean during their menstrual period and were expected to live in seclusion. So this unnamed woman with the flow of blood was flouting the Law (Jn 19:7).

She lived in a man's world, and the purity ritual laws that forbade contact were there to safeguard men more than any such principle.[40] Since this woman had been ill for twelve years, she would have been registered as permanently unclean because she could not carry out the obligatory *mikveh* when the flow of blood ceased and she would then return to normal social relations and interaction with others in the community. If married, her illness was grounds for divorce. If single, she would not have been eligible for marriage. In short, she was a social outcast and an embarrassment. She *"had suffered much under many physicians, and had spent all that she had, and was no better but rather grew worse"* (Mk 5:26). Having been brought to her knees, metaphorically speaking, she turned to Jesus.

This was a daring act as she was barred from public places. Cowardice asks, "Is this a safe thing to do?" Faith, on the other hand, says, "Go for it." This woman had the seed of faith. Even so, for her to simply touch the hem of his garment would defile Jesus and lay him open to accusations of breaking the Law by his enemies—the scribes, Pharisees, and Sadducees. They were already tackling him and carried a register of his words and deeds that displeased them. They would present this in evidence against him at the appropriate moment. However, the woman sneaked up to the hem of his cloak in the middle of a crowd of people. She was healed instantly and when Jesus reacted to what had happened, she was obliged to stand in full view of the crowd. Scripture tells us that when Jesus reacted to her touch, she *"came [forward] in fear and trembling"* (Mk 5:33). Perhaps she was frightened because she had involved Jesus in ritual uncleanness and given the Pharisees present another piece of evidence to add to their register, or perhaps it was due to the miraculous effect that had been worked in her.[41] Maybe she was scared that having touched Jesus surreptitiously he would be angry with her.[42] Perhaps she feared lest the crowd should react with hostility and attack her.

It is reasonable to assume that, having knowledge of Jesus and his works, she also knew of the reactions of the various consecrated groups to his ministry. She had reason to be afraid for her own and for his safety. Despite all this, it is most likely that she was overcome with awe at being healed. The important point in the story is that she had recognized her God in Jesus and was rewarded with healing. Desperation had brought her to faith. She was changed forever. Jesus affirmed her as *"Daughter."* Among the discipleship she was recognized as a daughter of the Church and in consequence her story was preserved for the edification of all future generations. As a grateful member of the faith community, it is reasonable to believe that she was among the group of women from Galilee who traveled with him from Galilee to Jerusalem (Mt 27:55).

In a delicate but clever way, Mark identifies this woman's sufferings with those of Jesus in his prediction of his own sufferings when he writes *"And he began to teach them that the Son of Man must suffer many things"* (Mk 8:31). In identifying the woman's situation and suffering with that of Jesus, he points out that *"she had suffered much under many physicians."* He draws a further parallel when he points out that the woman *"told him the whole truth"* (Mk 5:33), and states that Jesus was recognized by those who sought to trap, condemn, and kill him as a man of truth: *"And they came and said to him, 'Teacher, we know that you are true, and care for no man; for you do not regard the position of men, but truly teach the way of God'"* (Mk 12:14). Clearly, when Jesus saw genuine suffering he was reminded in a very poignant and vivid way of what he himself was experiencing.

His vision of what lay ahead was also heightened. In a unique way he felt and claimed the woman's pain. She confessed publicly that she was the one who caused power to go out from Jesus (Lk 8:47). In so doing she was witnessing to her faith and calling others to faith. A careful reading of Luke's Gospel illustrates that witness to faith was the true mark of genuine discipleship. Consequently, it is most reasonable to believe that this unnamed woman became a member of the group of most loyal followers of Jesus and that she was one of *"the women who had followed him from Galilee [who] stood at a distance and saw these things"* (Lk 23:49).

While it is true that evidence by a woman was not accepted as valid in Judaism, the testimony and integrity of this woman was acclaimed by Jesus himself in the most endearing terms. He stood for equality and social justice, and he recognized and affirmed faith, authenticity, and humility as qualities of those who aspired to promote and inherit the kingdom.

Discrimination and legalism were alien to him because he was committed to bringing compassion and mercy to all God's people and especially those, like this woman, who were most vulnerable, and who were either under threat or afraid. His was a mission of liberation and resurrection to new life as is evidenced by the fact that this woman and all the other women who approached him went away renewed, restored, and transformed. "The women Jesus encounters move into the Church's memory from an environment that barely distinguishes them as shadows."[43] This woman, too, was of no importance to the religious leaders of her day. Yet she is one of our foremothers in the faith who has stood out in the pages of Scripture for more than two thousand years. Her story continues to inspire and to challenge us because it made its own contribution to the book of evidence kept by Jesus' enemies in preparation for his passion and death.

Reflection

The woman had suffered an incomprehensible level of embarrassment, isolation, and mental agony for years. Despite this, she had either held fast to her faith in God or come to faith because of it. This faith led her eventually to Jesus and freed her from her physical ailment. He did not comment on her spiritual state, so it is clear that she was a virtuous woman who lived a holy, compassionate, and caring life despite being ostracized and infirm.

Having healed her, Jesus did not allow her to escape into the crowd. He was on a mission, a mission that meant constantly reaching out to others regardless of their place on the social ladder. Healings were intended not only to restore the infirm to health but also to energize the faith of all those present at the time. Each healing act carried out by Jesus was an invitation to relationship; it resulted in transformation, communication, affirmation, and thanksgiving. It was a true participation in the Eucharist.

When Jesus called for the one who had taken power from him to acknowledge their action and his response to it, he was not aiming to degrade or humiliate. No. He was inviting the person and all others in the crowd into a relationship. He was there to commend faith and to restore harmony in the social, emotional, spiritual, and physical lives of all those who were willing to reach out to touch God and to allow themselves to be embraced in mercy.

There is no way of naming the woman's illness. All we know is that she carried a huge cross for a very long period of time. As in Jesus' own case, this anonymous woman lived a life of agony. Like his, hers was an ongoing pain. In her day, modern health medicines were unheard of, so we do not know whether she was the victim of an irregular cycle, an early or an extended menopause, or some unique and undiagnosable condition. What we do know is that she trusted in Divine Providence and that her faith was rewarded, renewed, and enhanced.

During Lent, this woman tells us that in order to be true disciples we must not worry about giving things up as children do, but instead we should touch our God afresh by taking on some of the devotional practices that we have let slip, such as daily prayer and the sacrament of reconciliation. Furthermore, she encourages us to look again at our own values, our attitudes to stratification and oppression in society, and our feelings toward those who contract dangerous illnesses such as AIDS or any of the many sexually transmitted diseases that plague postmodern society.

> ✺ What is the hemorrhage we live with daily that continues to hurt us now, and what are we doing about it? Do we see it as our life shaper? What would we be doing and what kind of persons would we be if we did not have this particular agony to struggle with?

❧ Consider life over the years. Might the cross that has been weighing us down be an invitation to something wonderful? Might it be that which will ultimately shape us for a great future in God's service and the furtherance of the kingdom?

As the woman learned, there is no conversion or growth without the cross. If we did not have Good Friday, we would not have Easter Sunday. None of us wants to hemorrhage our way through life—whether that hemorrhage be the loss of a child, partner, marriage, consecrated or priestly commitment, parent, home, job, or promotion. But if we have suffered any one of these bereavements, perhaps our Lenten reflection on this woman's story will give us an opportunity to ask ourselves how the loss is affecting our lives.

❧ Has it made us bitter and judgmental? Has it made us hyperactive and, as a result, are we so busy trying to raise other people from their knees that we have no time to get down on our own? Has it the potential to enable us to touch Jesus afresh or maybe for the first time?

As people of faith or genuine seekers like the disciples on the way to Emmaus (Lk 24:13–32), we are most likely to recognize God at work in our lives when we are on our knees rather than when we are screaming in anger or apportioning blame to Divine Providence. We might like to live a life in which everything is carefully constructed and choreographed for our convenience, but that is not the model of creativity that our Creator embraced in the formless void into which the Spirit breathed life at the moment of Creation (Gen 1:2).

❧ Is it possible that during Lent this year we might discover that our crosses are invitation to us to allow the Spirit to breathe on our hemorrhage or formless void and heal us by bringing order into our chaos?

Wholeheartedly welcoming this graced period of passiontide has the potential to heal our hemorrhages, to liberate us from our prejudices, and to enable us to embrace compassionately those whose hemorrhaging addictions and lifestyles are different from ours. If we identify our true selves to Jesus, we will find that on Easter Sunday we will be able to stand tall in the crowd in church embracing the risen Christ in the Eucharist and in each other. There Jesus will greet each of us as a *"Daughter."*

The Crippled Woman Who Was Healed on the Sabbath

LUKE 13:10–17

IN CALLING FOR the death of Jesus, his enemies used his claims to higher authority as a reason for having him crucified. Nowhere did he make that claim more clearly than in the narrative relating to this daughter of Abraham.

> *"And ought not this woman, a daughter of Abraham whom Satan bound for eighteen years, be loosed from this bond on the sabbath day?"* (Lk 13:16)

Seeing him carry out an act of mercy and compassion for someone who prayed for healing and was a dedicated worshipper, the Pharisees had another point to add to their book of evidence recording Jesus' "breaches" of the Law and his misappropriation of power and authority. In keeping with belief at the time relating to illnesses that could not be diagnosed, the woman's condition was ascribed to *"a spirit"* (Lk 13:11). To the leader of the synagogue, the Pharisees, and the other official religious groups, this woman's condition was not automatically to be ascribed to Satan. She was known to observe the Sabbath laws and to reverence her God.

Scholars regard it as a little strange that Luke ascribes the woman's condition to Satan. Some attempt to explain the conundrum by saying that, "Jesus was locked in a life-and-death struggle with evil. The background is the world; humans are being used as pawns of the evil one."[44] However, because the healing took place on the Sabbath, and Jesus claimed authority over that day, he was pronounced guilty without any trial and with nobody to defend him except the woman who *"praised God,"* and her co-worshippers who rejoiced that she had been healed (Lk 13:13). He was alone with a mission that only he understood.

In some ways the story is reflective of a number of stories in the gospels relating to authority and the Sabbath, for example, the account given in Mark 3:1–6, relating to the healing of the man with the withered hand in the synagogue on the Sabbath. From this it is clear that observance of the Sabbath was a huge issue for the Jews, but just as they were skewed in their interpretation of the Law on adultery, they also had a double standard regarding legitimate work on the holy day (Mt 12:12; Mk 3:4; Lk 13:15; Lk 14:5; Jn 9:15–16). On each of these occasions, Jesus' opponents challenged his action and authority.

This woman stands in stark contrast not only to the leader of the synagogue whose "behaviour showed that he cared less for a crippled woman in his synagogue than for his farm animal,"[45] but to all the Pharisees, Sadducees, and the scribes. His interpretation of the Law as to when God could use divine power blinded him to the presence and power of God in front of him in his synagogue and to his own need for mercy. Jesus always challenged his opponents where it hurt most—in relation to their possessions. Like all leaders, this one would most certainly free a trapped animal on the Sabbath and how much more precious was a trapped human being in the eyes of God? (Lk 13:15).

By releasing a hostage from possible acute arthritis, degeneration of the spine, or some other unknown condition, Jesus was simply fulfilling the mission statement that he selected from Isaiah as the guiding vision of his ministry when he carried out his first teaching appointment in the synagogue at the beginning of his ministry (Lk 4:18–19). He was releasing a captive woman from the bond of evil and so mirroring the release of her ancestors from captivity in Babylon so many centuries earlier. He was also demonstrating to the Pharisees that women, too, had an equal right with men to their Jewish heritage. It was not the reserve of men to be healthy or to receive healing. For Jesus the Sabbath was most truly celebrated when works of mercy were carried out and when the dignity of women was celebrated.

"The miracle, in this instance, is an expression of his authority and power."[46] Jesus was not only reinterpreting the Law (Deut 5:12) in terms of providing humanitarian guidelines for the leader of the synagogue, the scribes, the Pharisees, and the leaders of all religious groups, but he was also defining how the Christian Sabbath might best be observed in the future. In his presence the woman spoke up in praise of God. Her dignity had been restored. Now she was claiming her right as a woman and a member of God's covenant community to speak in the assembly of the synagogue.

His response to the indignation of the leader of the synagogue and his directive to all those present that *"There are six days on which work ought to be done; come on those days and be healed, and not on the sabbath day"* (Lk 13:14) was not directed only at the leader but at the entire assembly. They must not allow themselves to be swayed by the narrow-minded legalism of petty officials who were insecure with their own authority, their positions, and the truth and as a result blind to the pastoral needs of the most faithful and loyal worshippers in their congregations. Healing and reconciliation were, Jesus taught, gifts of God and they were offered freely to anyone, at any time, who chose to turn in faith to the one who is mercy.

Jesus had liberated the woman but not without a cost to her and to himself. It left him in agony knowing that another piece of unjust evidence had been stacked up against him because he dared to challenge false interpretations of the Law and to heal on the Sabbath.

Reflection

Nobody asked Jesus to reach out in mercy and compassion to this unfortunate woman. In his love he saw the genuine desire and need of one of God's daughters to be healed. He had come to free all women from the captivity created by the Fall (Gen 3:1–19). He also saw an opportunity to give a teaching to a large assembly of the people and their consecrated leaders regardless of what their reaction might be to him. So totally focused was he on the kingdom that he overlooked the mental and emotional suffering that he would be forced to undergo from the Pharisees, scribes, and elders because of his interpretation of the Law and his compassion for suffering humanity. He had a mission, and fear was not going to deflect him from it.

This story presents us with a member of his congregation who was female and a spiritual leader who was male. The woman was a victim and disabled. The man was in authority, healthy, and unaware of the desperation of the woman. Jesus entered the scene. He cured her and challenged him. He affirmed her and condemned him. The woman became a cause for rejoicing and celebration. The leader folded up in shame.

This woman's faithful attendance in the synagogue week after week shows that she was a genuinely religious person who accepted her deformity believing that the Potter who created the clay from which she had been formed had unique plans for her. Like many a woman who suffers an injury or a threatening illness she prayed for healing. Like so many women, too, who have been cured at Lourdes or as a result of the intercession of some saint, she was eternally grateful for the restoration of her health. She stands out in Scripture as a model of submission to the will of God, of hope in divine compassion, and of faith in divine providence. Her reward is clear: Jesus saw her with his eyes, called her from his heart, and touched her with his hand, and she was healed to the jubilation of all in the assembly except the leader who should have been her advocate and pastor.

- If we are pastors or leaders in community, how do we deal with the obvious physical, social, emotional, and spiritual needs of our people? Are we genuinely compassionate and ever ready to join in prayer partnerships, or do we allow time and the business of life to blur the pain and so leave those in agony to journey alone?

- The leader of the synagogue was angered when he saw Jesus affirmed by the people for having healed the woman. How do we react when those we consider to be inferior to us in role or social status are acknowledged and praised?

- Jesus was unhappy with the rigid interpretation of Sabbath observance as practiced by teachers of the Law. This Lent let us ask ourselves: if he came physically among us today, how would he react to our liberal interpretation of the Christian Sabbath? There are the long sleep-ins and having no time for worship, the unnecessary work carried out, the shop-till-you-drop mentality, and the lack of time for the family to share a meal and talk to each other. Then there is the trend among teenagers and younger children of "sleepovers" in friends' houses, which means there is no time for worship on Saturday evening and, having partied most of the night, little inclination from the young to attend worship on Sunday.

✍ Do we realize that Lent is a great time for us to examine our use of the Sabbath and maybe to make a commitment to renewing our relationship with our God through metaphorical "sleep-ins" and "sleepovers" in partnership with our local community in worship?

Those of us Christians who must work on a Sunday are hostages to necessity. We are blame-free and to be admired for our stamina and dedication to ensuring that our bills are paid, our children are clothed, that there is food on our tables, that we share with the poor, and that the needs of the community are met. Those who choose to work at the expense of family quality time and relationships are allowing that which should support family to exclude it. In so doing we are also hostages, but hostages to our own avarice.

✍ This Lent might we reflect on the leader, the victim, and on Jesus' teaching in the story we have just looked at and allow them to help us in our prioritizing?

It might enrich our reflections on Jesus' reaction to the woman who was crippled and when making important decisions relating to our Sabbath if we remind ourselves as we make our way along our Lenten journey that when it came to making decisions, Jesus did not ask himself the following questions:

- ❧ "Will the action I take or the decision I make benefit me socially?"

- ❧ "Will I gain financially by acting in this way?"

- ❧ "Will my friends approve of this decision or this action?"

- ❧ "Is the decision I am about to make or the action I am about to take political?" No. His actions made their own statement: "Compassion is my only response."

Mary the Mother of Jesus

JOHN 19:26–27

FINALLY, WE TURN to Mary the mother of Jesus to whom John gives a very special place in the passion narratives and who is also accounted for by name in Matthew and Luke. Mary's roles in the passion were those of victim, mother of the accused, the condemned, and the victim of Jerusalem's and Rome's greatest recorded act of injustice.

> *When Jesus saw his mother, and the disciple whom he loved standing near, he said to his mother, "Woman, behold, your son!" Then he said to the disciple, "Behold, your mother!" And from that hour the disciple took her to his own home* (Jn 19:26–27).

The mother of Jesus was in a unique position in ministry and in her son's life. Her roles were to be transformed and transcended for her by her son before he took his last breath. Thereafter, she, like Mary Magdalene and the other women disciples, was to have an apostolic position. She was commissioned to become the mother of the new household of God.[47] She, not Mary Magdalene, would nurture the infant church in a unique and generative way.

Despite this change and challenge, she continued her domestic duties as mother and friend to all those in the discipleship and beyond to all who needed her support. It is because of this that she is so appealing to all mothers down through history. She was a simple, unassuming woman who made her home and her family her priority. The "yes" she gave to Gabriel at the annunciation remained firmly implanted in her heart and was lived out daily in her life regardless of the challenges and the lot that life dealt to her. She knew that the hand she had been dealt in life was less important than her response to it and the positive use that she made of it in a life of faith and mercy.

She had been present at Cana and she had encouraged and witnessed her son's first miracle. Now she was present again to witness him taking his last breath on the cross. The whole of his ministry had been sandwiched between these two events. At Cana she saw him turn water into wine and so give new life and joy to all those who were present. The wedding banquet was a symbol of the messianic age as illustrated by Luke 14:15–24. So, at Cana Mary witnessed something that had an eternal significance. On Calvary she saw blood and water flow from his side, symbols of new life and its sustainment, as he died. A new age had dawned. He had given his own blood as the new wine of the Eucharist to all those who would accept it in discipleship. Cana had merely prepared the way for Calvary. Mary was an integral part of both.

She, like any mother, probably did not understand what was happening to and being required from her. Moving from the familiar to the unfamiliar is never easy, as any of us who have moved to a new residence know only too well, and so does any child who has moved to a new school or young person who has moved away from home. Moving from one place to another, and from one mindset to another, takes time and involves struggle, pain, loss, and a period of grieving. There is a process involved here. The positive working through of that process leads to growth, a new life, and a new vision.

Mary had been surprised to the point of being shattered when Gabriel appeared to her and invited her to become Jesus' mother (Lk 1:26–38). She continued in that uncertain emotional state as she journeyed to her cousin Elizabeth, only to have her emotions integrated peacefully with her intellect when Elizabeth affirmed her in her decision and in her new role as mother of the son of God (Lk 1:43).

As she journeyed from Jerusalem to Calvary, Mary was a broken woman who became crushed to the point of paralysis, as she witnessed her only son crucified and dying as though he were a common criminal. That state was transformed when Jesus singled her out and commissioned her and the beloved disciple to form the heart of the church and to ensure that his work continued. Through being his mother she had always been mother of the Church, but now he officially commissioned her in that role (see *Catechism of the Catholic Church*, 963–965). Just as she had to journey to discover the precise meaning of Gabriel's message, so too, she had to take time and space with the disciples back in Jerusalem after the crucifixion, resurrection, and ascension in order to work out all the events of her son's life before she was, holistically, in a position to understand her new role in a discipleship called the Church.

In time Mary would have understood her new role and labored through prayer and service to be a source of life and joy to all who allowed her to support them in mercy. Mary was Jesus' penultimate extravagant gift in love to the discipleship. His ultimate gift would be his own life, and that he was about to gift to the discipleship and to all who joined the partnership in the future.

What was commissioned by Jesus on the cross was surely a discipleship of equals under the patronage of Mary and John, while allowing Peter to carry out the leadership role given to him by Jesus in the words, *"And I tell you, you are Peter, and on this rock I will build my church, and the powers of death shall not prevail against it"* (Mt 16:18).

> *Jesus' gift of love is to be replicated in relationships between disciples. The woman moved from being only his mother to the mother; in a comparable way, the disciples proceed from identification as "his" to belonging to a new family in Church.*[48]

We are left to wonder if the male disciples ever embraced this discipleship of equals in its fullness. Has it, even today, been realized? If we believe that it has not, we need to consider ways of helping it forward. It is our duty to work to ensure that women and men carry out the mission of Jesus in a partnership of equality, justice, and mercy. That Mary's role is recognized is certain, but it is worth reminding ourselves that for many centuries she was, metaphorically speaking, treated almost as one of the disappeared by the Western Church.

Reflection

As he hung on the cross, Jesus transformed his mother's role by elevating it to the new leadership position of mother of the Church. In recognizing his mother's unique contribution to mission he was affirming all women who stand daily beneath a cross. They, too, are guarantors of the good news. They, too, are witnesses to the crucifixion, death, and resurrection of the Messiah. Mary had to pick herself up and go forward as mother, not to Jesus alone, but to the many sons and daughters she inherited because of him. She had to be strong for them. Herein lies a challenge for all women who feel broken and helpless or who feel that life has dealt them an unfair hand in, maybe, the loss of a child through an accident, murder, suicide, or in a sudden death.

Mary did not consider the justice of the hand she had been dealt. No, she accepted it and set about "trading" with it. She realized that while it is essential to grieve, process pain, and take time and space to mourn, it is also crucial to accept what the good God has in his wisdom allowed to befall each of his children. And having accepted and embraced it, it is appropriate to grasp the hand of Mary, and to make every possible effort to rise to the challenge and go forward in faith, hope, and love.

- Are we truly children who understand the passion and death of Christ because we have embraced it in our Lenten pilgrimage and begun to embrace it in our own lives?

- How do we accept the "hand that has been dealt" to us in life? Do we strive to respond positively to our lot and work to make it fruitful, generative, and a basis from which we can grow, develop new vision, and be more merciful to others who are suffering?

- Are we willing to strive to forget ourselves and reach out to those who may be more vulnerable, less well able to cope, and in need of a structured support system, as in "Woman behold your Son"?

Jesus initiated his eucharistic ministry at Cana at the request of Mary and brought it to a conclusion in her presence on Calvary.

- What part does the Eucharist play in our spirituality and in our devotions to Mary as we journey through Lent with a view to renewal? Do we witness to its importance in our lives in ways that make it attractive to others?

Conclusion

THE PASSION OF Jesus, the women of the passion, and our Lent are about extravagant giving in mercy—the giving of self in service. They are about the triumph of truth, justice, self-worth, and mercy in ministry. These are virtues in which Jesus was grounded and in which he schooled the women who, as our representatives, became his partners.

Only when we acknowledge our own need for mercy and our duty to promote justice, recognize our worth, and are comfortable with ourselves are we able to be there for him who was, and who is, there for us. Then our vision will be unclouded. We'll be free to live holistically and serve unconditionally. Only when we learn to be merciful to ourselves are we free to be mercy for others. Then, like the women of the passion, we will have learned to see and respond to the reality of our surroundings; we will have allowed him to remove darkness, insecurity, and our egocentricity. Often we minister to what we decide other people need without allowing them any input. Sometimes by just being present with them our silent anointing partnership can achieve more than can delivering profound theories and doctrines relating to faith, ethics, and morals.

Let us make this Lent a time to look into our own hearts and examine our motives and intentions. Then, purified by the waters of repentance, each day will become Easter. We will become an Easter people with the right to sing "Alleluia." Only then, and in reverence for *"this man's blood"* (Mt 27:24) and the women of the passion, will the ointment that we immerse ourselves in, and use to anoint fellow Christians, be that of warm, lubricating, life-giving, and extravagant mercy.

Endnotes

1. Pope John Paul II. Letter to Women, no 3, 1995.
2. Mary Anne Getty Sullivan. *Women in the New Testament.* Liturgical Press, Collegeville, Minnesota, 2001, p. 212.
3. John L. McKenzie, S.J. *Dictionary of the Bible.* Geoffrey Chapman, London, 1972, p. 35.
4. Ibid., p. 216.
5. Sue and Larry Richards. *Every Woman in the Bible.* Thomas Nelson Publishers, Nashville, Tennessee, 1999, p. 197.
6. Edited by Raymond E. Brown, S.S., Joseph A. Fitzmyer, S.J., and Roland E. Murphy, O.Cam. *The New Jerome Biblical Commentary.* Prentice Hall, Englewood Cliffs, New Jersey, 1990, 1968, p. 669.
7. Ibid.
8. Stephen Barton. *People of the Passion.* Triangle, SPCK, London, 1994, p. 3.
9. Herbert Lockyer. *All the Women of the Bible.* Zondervan Publications, Grand Rapids, Michigan, 1967, p. 226.
10. Sue and Larry Richards. *Every Woman in the Bible.* Thomas Nelson Publishers, Nashville, Tennessee, 1999, p. 200.
11. Edited by Raymond E. Brown, S.S., Joseph A. Fitzmyer, S.J., and Roland E. Murphy, O.Cam. *The New Jerome Biblical Commentary.* Prentice Hall, Englewood Cliffs, New Jersey, 1990, 1968, p. 671.
12. Ibid., pp. 671–672

13. Mary Anne Getty Sullivan. *Women in the New Testament.* Liturgical Press, Collegeville, Minnesota, 2001, p. 133.

14. Edith Dean. *All The Women of The Bible.* Harper Collins, New York, 1988, p. 205.

15. Richard Bauckham. *Gospel Women.* T&T Clark International, London, 2002, p. xxi.

16. Mary Anne Getty Sullivan. *Women in the New Testament.* Liturgical Press, Collegeville, Minnesota, 2001, p.118.

17. Herbert Lockyer. *All the Women of the Bible.* Zondervan Publications, Grand Rapids, Michigan, 1967, p. 235.

18. Edited by Raymond E. Brown, S.S., Joseph A. Fitzmyer, S.J., and Roland E. Murphy, O.Cam. *The New Jerome Biblical Commentary.* Prentice Hall, Englewood Cliffs, New Jersey, 1990, 1968, p. 719.

19. Edited by Raymond E. Brown, S.S., Joseph A. Fitzmyer, S.J., and Roland E. Murphy, O.Cam. *The New Jerome Biblical Commentary.* Prentice Hall, Englewood Cliffs, New Jersey, 1990, 1968, p. 965.

20. John L McKenzie, S.J. *Dictionary of the Bible.* Geoffrey Chapman, London, 1972, p.14.

21. Mary Anne Getty Sullivan. *Women in the New Testament.* Liturgical Press, Collegeville, Minnesota, 2001, p. 103.

22. Virginia Stem Owens. *Daughters of Eve.* Navpress, Colorado Springs, Colorado, 1995, p. 126.

23. Mary Anne Getty Sullivan. *Women in the New Testament.* Liturgical Press, Collegeville, Minnesota, 2001, p. 104.

24. John J Mcllon. *Forty Days Plus Three.* Liturgical Press, Collegeville, Minnesota, 1989, p. 55.

25. Joseph Cardinal Ratzinger. Letter to the Bishops of the Catholic Church on the Collaboration of Men and Women in the Church and in the World. Vatican Press, 2004, III no 13.

26. Mary Anne Getty Sullivan. *Women in the New Testament.* Liturgical Press, Collegeville, Minnesota, 2001, p. 96.

27. Denis McBride, C.Ss.R. *Seasons of the Word: Reflections on the Sunday Readings.* Redemptorist Publications, Alton, Hants. 1991, p. 83.

28. Richard Bauckham. *Gospel Women.* T&T Clark International, London, 2002, p. 236.

29. Edith Dean. *All The Women of The Bible.* Harper Collins, New York, 1988, p. 371.

30. Sue and Larry Richards. *Every Woman in the Bible.* Thomas Nelson Publishers, Nashville, Tennessee, 1999, p.186.

31. Mary Anne Getty Sullivan. *Women in the New Testament.* Liturgical Press, Collegeville, Minnesota, 2001, p. 111.

32. Edith Dean. *All The Women of The Bible.* Harper Collins, New York, 1988, p. 203.

33. Herbert Lockyer. *All the Women of the Bible.* Zondervan Publications, Grand Rapids, Michigan, 1967, p. 100.

34. Mary Anne Getty Sullivan. *Women in the New Testament.* Liturgical Press, Collegeville, Minnesota, 2001, p. 185.

35. Herbert Lockyer. *All the Women of the Bible.* Zondervan Publications, Grand Rapids, Michigan, 1967, p. 106.

36. Ibid., p. 150.

37. Edith Dean. *All The Women of The Bible.* Harper Collins, New York, 1988, p. 193.

38. Richard Bauckham. *Gospel Women.* T&T Clark International, London, 2002, p. 203.

39. Ibid., p. 209.

40. Mary Anne Getty Sullivan. *Women in the New Testament.* Liturgical Press, Collegeville, Minnesota, 2001, p. 69.

41. Edited by Raymond E. Brown, S.S., Joseph A. Fitzmyer, S.J., and Roland E Murphy, O.Cam. *The New Jerome Biblical Commentary.* Prentice Hall, Englewood Cliffs, New Jersey, 1990, 1968, p. 608.

42. Richard Bauckham. *Gospel Women.* T&T Clark International, London, 2002, p. 292.

43. Mary Anne Getty Sullivan. *Women in the New Testament.* Liturgical Press, Collegeville, Minnesota, 2001, p. 43.

44. Ibid., p.83.

45. Sue and Larry Richards. *Every Woman in the Bible.* Thomas Nelson Publishers, Nashville, Tennessee, 1999, p. 165.

46. Mary Anne Getty Sullivan. *Women in the New Testament.* Liturgical Press, Collegeville, Minnesota, 2001, p. 81.

47. Stephen Barton. *People of the Passion.* Triangle, SPCK, London, 1994, p, 65.

48. Mary Anne Getty Sullivan. *Women in the New Testament.* Liturgical Press, Collegeville, Minnesota, 2001, p. 230.